Praise for Powered by

"If you're committed to wo   . mean really working
with them in every respect, th,   ...essy beauty of their activism—
Powered by Girl is an essential re

—Loretta Ross, cofounder of SisterSong

"Highlighting the collective dimensions of girls' activism, *Powered by Girl* is an important corrective to over-simplified discussions of girls' empowerment. Brown's passionate call for intergenerational collaboration engages with the challenges and rewards of this kind of activism, demonstrates a profound respect for girls' knowledge and expertise, and asks all the right questions about how adults can better support girls in the struggle for a more just world."

—Jessica K. Taft, author of *Rebel Girls:*
Youth Activism and Social Change Across the Americas

"Behind every 'exceptional' girl is . . . a movement! Kudos to Lyn Mikel Brown for identifying the architecture that lifts up the next generation of feminists!"

—Jennifer Baumgardner and Amy Richards,
authors of *Manifesta* and *Grassroots*

"If you teach, mentor, or work with girls, you need to read *Powered by Girl*. Full of stories and strategies, it's a must-read manual for nurturing agency, sisterhood, and critical consciousness in girl activists. Adults will learn when to step up and when to step back, how to cultivate inclusiveness and truth telling among girls, and how to develop the most fertile conditions for girl activism to flourish."

—Rachel Simmons, author of *Odd Girl Out* and *The Curse of the Good Girl*

"I am a *huge* fan of Lyn Mikel Brown's; her partnerships with girls and support of their activism are nothing short of revolutionary. *Powered by Girl* explains how she joined forces across generations to make change—and, even better, how we can too!"

—Peggy Orenstein, author of *Girls & Sex:*
Navigating the Complicated New Landscape

"Brown offers us a powerful and urgent critique of the media-generated 'kick-ass girl,' a mythical girl who supposedly needs no one but herself to change the world. Behind the scenes, Brown shows us how real girls and women can truly kick some ass by working together on jointly constructed actions for social justice. An essential read for those who want to create a more just and humane world and want girls and women to lead the way. Read it right here, right now!"

—Niobe Way, author of *Deep Secrets:*
Boys' Friendship and the Crisis of Connection

"In this bold, inspiring book, Lyn Mikel Brown investigates the realities and possibilities of intergenerational activism—and does not shrink from the challenges. A blueprint for intergenerational feminist work, *Powered by Girl* offers multiple strategies for adult women to build hopeful, respectful activist relationships with girls, all the while acknowledging the complexities of grassroots politics today."

—Anita Harris, Research Professor,
Institute for Citizenship and Globalisation, Deakin University

"The development of honest dialogues between adult allies and girls is the key to social change—and recognizing that girls are the most qualified experts of their experiences is critical to their activism. Lyn Mikel Brown's book accurately captures the benefits—and challenges—of how to nurture our next generation of change agents."

—Clarice Bailey and Charlotte Jacobs, Girls Justice League

"*Powered by Girl* is a godsend for everyone who parents or works with girls. Girls are passionate about making the world a better place. But when they try to do so, obstacles appear that adults need to help with. Lyn Mikel Brown shows us how and challenges us to go far beyond vague good intentions by building genuine, respectful, mutually trusting relationships that succeed in making change both out in the world and inside ourselves."

—Nancy Gruver, founder, New Moon Girls

"*Powered by Girl* is the essential manual for anyone working with young activists—from youth workers to seasoned mentors. Lyn Mikel Brown presents the necessary skills for adult allies to be supportive and effective backseat drivers while girls do the steering."

—Wendy Lesko, president of Youth Activism Project
and cofounder of School Girls Unite

"In an increasingly commodified feminist movement, *Powered by Girl* offers insight into how girls and young women can reimagine a movement rooted in political activism, and gives activists the tools to do so in an intergenerational and inclusive way."

—Julie Zeilinger, founding editor, FBomb

"*Powered by Girl* is a compelling narrative and rationale for feminist intergenerational practices *with girls*, dismantling ageist models of girls' programming and making visible the diverse ways coalitions of girls and their allies are pushing forward a new feminist agenda. An important book for all interested in girls' studies and girls' activism."

—Amy Rutstein-Riley, PhD, MPH, principal investigator
of The Girlhood Project at Lesley University

Powered by Girl

A Field Guide for Supporting Youth Activists

Lyn Mikel Brown

BEACON PRESS
BOSTON

BEACON PRESS
Boston, Massachusetts
www.beacon.org

Beacon Press books
are published under the auspices of
the Unitarian Universalist Association of Congregations.

19 18 17 16   8 7 6 5 4 3 2 1

This book is printed on acid-free paper that meets the uncoated paper
ANSI/NISO specifications for permanence as revised in 1992.

Text design and composition by Kim Arney

Some names of girls mentioned in this work have
been changed to protect their identities.

Library of Congress Cataloging-in-Publication Data
Names: Brown, Lyn Mikel, author.
Title: Powered by girl : a field guide for supporting youth activists / Lyn Mikel Brown.
Description: Boston : Beacon Press, [2016] | Includes bibliographical references.
Identifiers: LCCN 2016012869 (print) | LCCN 2016020310 (ebook) |
ISBN 9780807094600 (paperback) | ISBN 9780807094617 (ebook)
Subjects: LCSH: Girls—Political activity. | Girl volunteers. | Social action. |
Community development. | BISAC: SOCIAL SCIENCE / Volunteer Work. |
SOCIAL SCIENCE / Children's Studies. | EDUCATION / Parent Participation.
Classification: LCC HQ799.2.P6 B76 2016 (print) | LCC HQ799.2.P6 (ebook) |
DDC 320.4083—dc23
LC record available at https://lccn.loc.gov/2016012869

TO MY WILLFUL, LOVING,
AND ALWAYS ENTERTAINING
DAUGHTER, MAYA

Contents

Digging Deep

By all appearances, the stars are aligned for young feminists. Armed with a well-honed sense of irony, an inventive amalgam of online and on-the-ground activism, and an intersectional lens, girl activists are getting it done. There's no denying the power of the feminist blogosphere or girls' and young women's use of a rich array of digital platforms to connect, rant, strategize, and land the movement. Girls are increasingly critical of media and marketers hell-bent on inventing and then profiting from their anxieties and desires; they've stayed ahead of corporate shibboleths by culture jamming and pushing back on efforts to sell them on personal failure of various kinds. As pop culture icons and political leaders alike begin to proclaim their feminism, there is an enlivened and palpable sense of possibility.

That possibility has taken hold in creative grassroots organizations, programs, and campaigns across the country, where girls are developing collective approaches to social-change work every day online and in their communities and schools. But popular media feed an American public that has, as English professor Wendy Hesford says, an "insatiable appetite for the *exceptional individual*,"[1] and so only a very few "special" girls will make it on the public radar screen. Girls like Madison Kimrey, who at age twelve founded NC

Youth Rock to protest voting-restriction laws targeting young people and minorities; fourteen-year-old Julia Bluhm, who demanded *Seventeen* magazine no longer photoshop girls' faces and bodies; and eleven-year-old Marley Dias, who launched a #1000BlackGirl-Books campaign, are lifted out of the relationships, support systems, and communities that enabled their remarkable work and celebrated as "creators of their own identities and life chances,"[2] living examples of the neoliberal vision of the individual as entrepreneur of the self.[3] They are model citizens, defined, ironically, by their lack of participation in any political community.

When girls with dreams and demands fueled by social injustice enter the fun house of popular media, they exit as the current "it" girls, the latest desirable commodity.

And activism is the new fashion accessory. Like the stars in celebrity magazines, girls with a cause are "Just like us!" which means, in pop culture vernacular, that they, too, are vulnerable, uncertain, and prone to bad hair days. They are strong and smart—and nonthreatening. "Lena Dunham the Activist," *Elle* announces, "is nothing if not polite . . . a blond ball of smiles and eye contact."[4] And "Transgender Teen Activist Jazz Jennings," *Seventeen* gushes, is just a girl struggling to fit in, inspiring other girls to discover "the Confidence to Be YOU."[5] Political dissent is serious fun and kind of glamorous. "Meet the Women Who Created #BlackLivesMatter," *Cosmo* announces, as Patrisse Cullors, Alicia Garza, and Opal Tometi grace the magazine's "Fun Fearless 50" list.[6]

This girl-activist makeover has a déjà vu feel, eerily reminiscent of '90s Girl Power, when media and marketers bypassed hip-hop feminism's call for solidarity and respect altogether and set their sights on transforming the largely white Riot Grrrl rebellion into a glittery wasteland of girly consumerism. Girl Power '90s style was exploitable, explains gender professor Marnina Gonick, because it resonated "with an image of the new ideal feminine subject demanded by neoliberalism," a self-determined (white, middle-class) girl, "assertive, dynamic, and unbound from the constraints of passive femininity."[7]

While no longer new, this ideal is more entrenched than ever. As present-day girl-fueled activism extends through communities and rises in visibility and impact, it is vulnerable to the same trajectory,[8] the same whitewashing, and the same denuding of political potential and effective public dissent. That girls and women of color like Jennings, Cullors, and Dias are included this time around doesn't alter the basic DNA. Girl activism as a commodity, as the domain of the individual special girl, channels attention away from social and structural inequalities and toward self-improvement and self-promotion.

"Girl Power commerce"[9] may look less like "fix yourself" these days and more like "love yourself," but there's no mistaking "the pernicious kind of lifestylism"[10] infused in current "fempowerment" marketing campaigns that tell us to "stop telling girls that they're weak, encourage them to get into STEM fields, quit apologizing for ourselves, and remember that we're damn good-looking just how we are."[11] These are better messages, for sure, but the onus is still on us. If we're told we can get into STEM fields, then it's our fault if we don't. The problem is not the systemic barriers pushing us out, it's our lack of self-confidence and initiative. This is just a different version of the same thing, and if we buy it, we'll ensure once again a Girl Power that doesn't actually empower girls.

The definition of crazy, as they say, is doing the same thing over and over again and expecting different results. Contemporary girls leadership programs are crazy-making; they are, by and large, simply '90s self-esteem-improvement programs dressed for success. Most are designed to prepare girls to take their exceptional places in the halls of power and influence. They take their cue from a Sheryl Sandberg–inspired promise that those who dare to "lean in" will seamlessly move into productive lives and lucrative careers.[12] Any girl is capable of great success if she can overcome her fear of being exceptional and ask for what she wants. She'll need lots of final touches first, of course. She'll need to develop the right body language, a firmer handshake. She'll need to shed signs of uncertainty, relational attachments, and cultural baggage. She'll have to adjust her facial expressions, control her anger, control her laughter, control her hair, fix her loud talk, her "uptalk," her "vocal fry"[13]—her excess of any kind. And above all, she'll need a willing suspension of disbelief—that every girl who does these things well enough will succeed, that equality is a done deal, that the system is fair, and that personal metamorphosis is the key. She'll need, in essence, to ignore what she knows about how the world really works.

In her critical response to Sandberg's *Lean In*, feminist social critic bell hooks examines the widespread circulation and seductive power of what British cultural theorist Angela McRobbie refers to as "faux feminism."[14] Contemporary girls are invited into an individualistic discourse of freedom and empowerment that ultimately undermines community and solidarity, both with other girls and with adults, creates barriers to girls' activism, and encourages girls to embrace and perpetuate the very conditions that serve to constrain, restrict, and subordinate them. Instead of leaning in to flawed systems, hooks challenges us to *dig deep*—to take on unjust systems and work together in coalition to imagine and build alternatives.

Digging deep requires not only that we think critically, that we look beneath the surface stories and explanations about the way things work, but that we engage in what theater artist Leah Lowe calls "critical generosity," a way of being "challenged, moved, and astonished" by others, of opening ourselves up to alternative ways of being and living in the world.[15] Digging deep demands self-reflection; that we consider how and why we participate in behaviors and systems we know can be harmful to ourselves and to others. It's hard work, exhausting, even, and so we need lots of support from others.

What it means for women to be challenged, moved, and astonished by girls has occupied me for some time. I often wonder what difference it might have made if women en masse had listened to and engaged girls' rage about sexual violence, racism, and homophobia in the 1990s. If women had talked with girls about sexual double standards and street harassment while watching Queen

Latifah's "U.N.I.T.Y." video; if women had read Riot Grrrl zines *with* girls rather than hand-wringing *Reviving Ophelia*–type books *about* them.[16] What if we trusted girls, saw them as experts on their lives, and engaged the messy, unpredictable process of relationship? What if we stepped into the complexity of girls' anger, sexual assertiveness, and rebellion—named the sources and together created a critical vocabulary and a way forward? Without romanticizing girls and young women at the turn of the twenty-first century, it's safe to say that many were naming and enacting feminist badassery. It's also safe to say that this made a lot of women very nervous, and the general response—programs designed to fix the symptoms and not the root causes—was not in girls' best interests.

Truth be told, it's not easy for women to partner with girls. It's a girl's generational right to disrupt the way things go. This is what it means to come of age—to ask questions, to point out contradictions, to negotiate a place in the world. Girls stake a generational claim both as young people and as girls, bringing with them new understandings and utopian visions. As women, we can and should invite them in, but this requires that we engage their resistance to things we hold dear, that we consent to live unsettled lives for the sake of their health and their best work, which means, of course, for the sake of their imagination, curiosity, critical thinking, and courage. Because open critique and public dissent are necessary to activism and social change, but are also deemed unfeminine and disruptive, extending this invitation to girls is especially difficult and complicated for women. Girls' critique is often turned on us, and fairly so.

But if we really want more girls who speak up and act out in the face of injustice in our schools and communities, we have to understand and invest in the conditions that support them. We have to appreciate what it means to partner with girls on a local level in ways that enable them to voice strong feelings and opinions, to think critically and grapple with the culture of power. We have to challenge the assumption that women and girls cannot work together—that women are too old and out of touch; that girls are too young and misinformed. Such falsehoods cut girls off from women's knowledge and strategic support, and cut women off from girls' creative brilliance, their energy, passion, and fun. In this book I explore what it means to dig deep into intergenerational activist work. In the first few chapters, I address the costs of our obsession with the exceptional girl and envision intergenerational activism as a pathway to social change. I explore the importance of understanding the conditions that invite girls' dissent and our tendency as women to shut down and turn off in the presence of girls' anger and resistance. And in addition to girl-fueled activism making the world a better place, I make a case for its health and developmental benefits.

Then, with the help of a diverse group of experienced activists, both girls and women, I outline a practice, a way of working, that cultivates dissent and enables intergenerational social-change work. Listening to activists reflect on their successes and failures, roadblocks, catalytic moments, the pleasures and dangers of working together, I consider the conditions necessary for effective working relationships—what it means to be aware, reflective, responsive, and intentional partners in girl-fueled social-change projects.

This field guide is not so much a how-*to*, then, as it is a how-to-*be*: how to be in relationship with girls—how to hear them, learn from them, enable and support their ideas, join them in their activism. The title denotes a very deliberate shift—from the static commodification of Girl Power to a dynamic process of activism fueled by, powered by, girls. Our capacity to challenge neoliberal versions of girlhood depends on offering conditions that enable girls to develop a critical vocabulary, to experience the explosive power of coalition work, to know how power and systems operate, to experience what it feels like to ask, advocate, demand, and not be alone. If we don't want to be part of another clever diversion and if we don't want to be the kind of adults girls struggle against, we need to step into this relational work and see where it takes us.

PART ONE

CULTIVATING DISSENT

When *Vogue* featured members of the feminist Russian punk group Pussy Riot who had served almost two years in prison for staging unauthorized guerrilla protests, the magazine announced how great it was that the band, "vilified in Russia for their fearless brand of activism," are "here . . . a cause célèbre."[1] Pussy Riot members perform in brightly colored balaclavas, which obscure their identities and serve to "oppose the very idea of using the female face" as a marketing tool.[2] In the *Vogue* story, under the headline "Enemy of the State," we see a photo of the two profiled women—stunning, both because they are not covered, but beautifully dressed and made up, and because their facial expressions and simple poses are startlingly passive. Beside the photo is a caption reading "Unchained Melody" with the following accompanying text:

> "Our minds are always on the prisons. We have friends who are still there, in disgusting conditions," says Masha (near right, in Michael Kors), who with Nadya (in Valentino) spent two years incarcerated in Russia. Hair, James Pecis; makeup, Benjamin Puckey.[3]

We know that girl-fueled activism can attract enormous public attention when the half-dozen media corporations that control 90 percent of what we read and watch want a piece of the action.[4] We can also expect that what makes it to our pages and screens will be ideologically loaded in self-interested ways—that is, in ways that undermine the truly radical and rebellious potential of girls' activism. How else do we explain the "she's so pretty when she's angry" remake of the girls and young women who are chosen by media to represent a cause?

This is a cover story, as in a cover-up or false story. Pussy Riot is likable, manageable. *Vogue* is edgy. Pussy Riot's story serves *Vogue*, but not the other way around. In chapter 1, I invite a healthy suspicion of the stories of girl activists we see in media. I begin with the cover-up story of activist Julia Bluhm's *Seventeen* magazine action, the erasure of layers of support she received from girls and women working with SPARK Movement, and her own frustration with the media version of events. I offer this as an instructive story about the radical potential of girl-fueled activism when situated in genuine coalition with girls and adults who dig deep together, and I offer this as a vitally important alternative to cover-ups that reward specialness, that channel desire, energy, and funds along well-worn neoliberal pathways.[5]

Individual girls' passion, courage, and intelligence are not in question. There is no doubt that even quite young girls are capable of the bravest acts, often suggesting the most ingenious solutions to social problems. It's wonderful when they get the attention they so deserve. But how we tell the story of their work is important. As progressive educator Herbert Kohl wrote in a wonderful article re-situating the story of Rosa Parks within a consciously planned series of actions, "the idea that only special people can create change is useful if you want to prevent mass movements and keep change from happening."[6] If we want real cultural change to take place, we need to appreciate how burying layers of support and focusing on an individual cause célèbre comes at the expense of girl activists everywhere.

So much depends on our ability and willingness as adults to openly question the thin veneer of lean-in versions of Girl Power and offer the opportunities and tools that enable young people to dig deep beneath stock phrases and simple solutions. In chapter 2, I consider what it means to *respect* girls' resistance, invoking, as bell hooks does in her book *Teaching to Transgress*, "the root meaning of the word, 'to look at'—each other, engage in acts of recognition with one another."[7] Really seeing girls, respecting them, means making every effort to understand the source of their open resistance; to question when their reactions to unfairness are shut down by others, pathologized, labeled as troublemaking; to openly challenge those who refer to girls' everyday rebellions in the face of what limits or hurts them as signs that they are bad or mean, that they lack resilience or self-esteem. Respect means entertaining the possibility that we don't always see clearly or hear well, and that we often mistake symptoms for causes.

Partnering with girls, especially across difference, demands our humility—our faith in the possibility of knowing, understanding, affirming the intersections and complexities of our identities in ways that open up space and possibilities. The hostilities and injustices aimed especially at girls of color, immigrant girls, queer girls, girls with disabilities, poor and working-class girls, require support from adults, especially within our homes and communities. Yet across the country women are teaching, guiding, and caring for girls who differ from them, and not doing it very well—often causing more harm than good. Chapter 2 invites those of us who work with girls, especially across difference, to reflect, to examine our privilege, to question our assumptions, to respect what girls can tell us about their lives so that we can better work in coalition with them to address the injustices and hurt they experience.

In chapter 3, I address the power and importance of intergenerational activism for girls' healthy development and for the betterment of our schools and communities. Girls' experiences and women's lives are inextricably linked. Listening to one another offers openings, new possibilities for involvement in the process of political change. Taking girls seriously is taking ourselves seriously. We close off their voices and visions, their anger, desire, sense of humor and satire, their dissent, at our own risk. Stepping into conversation and engaging in the rich, complex, and necessary work of feminist activism together is our best chance for a radical, creative, boundary-crossing interruption of self-interest and social injustice. Girls say they want these kinds of relationships with the women in their lives, but few will ever have the opportunity to experience them.

I've worked with wonderful young activists both online and on the ground in a variety of projects and campaigns. They are brilliant, passionate, and creative. But here's the thing: every one of them is or has been at one time engaged in some kind of intergenerational work, the depth and nature of which we will hear little. And yet, this work is the connective tissue, the textured enmeshments and in-betweens that matter most in our complicated and contradictory lives. Ensuring that this transformative work is visible, sharing the knowledge and creativity that arises in intergenerational coalitions, is a way to counter a false story that things change simply because someone suddenly speaks up or stands up in the moment.

The possibilities for creative resistance to systemic oppressions are all around us. "Sometimes it feels dangerous to be hopeful, to be angry, or to be creative," self-described agitator Carly Stasko says, "and yet we must create places for such expression in order to grow into ourselves and build the worlds we want."[8] If we really want a generation of girls who are engaged in political practice, we will meet them where they live, in our schools and communities. We will understand and invest in the conditions that support and enable them to connect with one another, voice strong feelings and opinions, think critically, oppose injustice, and grapple with the culture of power.

CHAPTER ONE

The Myth of the Special Girl

When Julia Bluhm was just fourteen, she wrote and posted an online petition with Change.org asking *Seventeen* magazine to agree to one non-photoshopped spread per month. She had heard one too many "I'm having a fat day" comments from the other girls in her ballet class, made the connection to her favorite teen magazine's propensity for featuring uberthin models, and decided to act. Her petition struck a public nerve and went viral. Julia made the rounds on national TV news shows, and dozens of blogs, newspapers, and magazines covered the story. In the end, eighty-six thousand people signed the petition. *Seventeen*'s executive director, Ann Shoket, raised a white flag in the form of a "Body Peace Treaty" in which the magazine agreed to a no-photoshop policy and committed to "celebrate every kind of beauty."[1] Newspaper headlines announced the victory: "Teen Julia Bluhm Convinces 'Seventeen' to Feature Realistic, Non-Airbrushed Models"[2] and "Maine Teen Wins Battle Against Seventeen on Photoshopped Images."[3]

In a country that worships superheroes and loves David and Goliath endings, it was a great story, an inspiring story. But it wasn't the real story.[4] Not even close. Missing in the avalanche of media celebrating Julia's specialness and singular success was the underlying reality: she was a well-trained, well-connected, and fully

supported member of a team of girl activists with SPARK Movement, a girl-fueled intergenerational activist organization working online and on the ground to ignite an antiracist gender-justice
movement.[5] While this added information might pluck Julia out
of the rarified air of self-made superstars, it affirms her as a very
smart and strategic young activist. As Julia explains: "I think collaboration has always been a key to leadership. Maybe there is one
person leading an action, but there are always a bunch of people
backing that person up and supporting them. With a bigger team
comes more resources, more people who hear about your action
and a bigger change. I think the most successful movements are
the result of teamwork."[6]

Julia had that bigger team. So did eight-year-old environmental activist and "kidpreneur" Maya Penn when she launched her
eco-fashion line; twelve-year-old anti-GMO activist Rachel Parent when she organized her first rally; and Andrea Gonzales, sixteen, and Sophie Houser, seventeen, when they invented Tampon
Run, a video game designed to break taboos around menstrua-
tion. Young activists don't just pop up fully formed and informed.
They are brave, passionate, and wide awake, yes, but they don't
possess unique activist genes. They have been the beneficiaries
of supportive environments, raised or educated or scaffolded by
people with deep skills. They have been enabled by socially conscious and committed adults who know how the system works,
who have shared their knowledge and resources, their time and
their connections, who have invested their energy and instilled in
youth what philosopher of education Maxine Greene calls a "passion for possibility."[7]

So what was the real story of the *Seventeen* magazine action? It
was a remarkable action initiated by a girl. This is true. But by a girl
whose activist tendencies were nurtured from a young age. Julia's
parents supported the "Lucky Lady Bugs" club she and her friends
started in third grade as a way to raise money for various community causes, hosting the group and driving them to their fund-
raising events. A fourth-grade public school teacher advised Julia's

Civil Rights Team, encouraging students to fight school-based bias and discrimination, and her sixth-grade guidance counselor helped Julia and her fellow students create a group called Student Body Advocates in support of their gender-nonconforming classmates. By seventh grade, Julia began to call herself an activist, telling me that she believed, as one of the so-called "good people" (her air quotes) in her school's social hierarchy, she had a responsibility to act in the face of unfairness. In middle school, Julia attended annual Girls Rock! conferences hosted by Hardy Girls Healthy Women, a feminist nonprofit in her community, where she learned about SPARK Movement. Once she joined the SPARKteam of girl activists, she participated in training on a range of issues, such as media literacy, intersectional feminism, antiracist movement building, blogging, petition development, and youth organizing.

Julia had all of this support, information, and experience at her disposal when she initiated her Change.org petition. Because the SPARKteam learned that effective petitions are often accompanied by engaging videos, Julia and teammate Izzy Labbe made a video of boys and girls in their junior high school commenting on a current issue of *Seventeen*, while Maya Brown, another team member, blogged about the progress of the petition, and the rest of the team facebooked, tweeted, and tumblred the news. SPARK alerted all sixty partner organizations, encouraging them to do the same.

Even with the support of this intergenerational coalition, Julia and the team were lucky. The timing was right. Her petition landed in the midst of news coverage on the sexualization of underage models, health concerns about too-thin models, and growing complaints and proposed legislation in France and England addressing the negative effects of photo editing on girls and young women. So when Change.org tested and sent the petition out to a broader audience, twenty-five hundred signatures quickly became tens of thousands. Given the possibility that Julia's petition could result in real and positive change, SPARK's executive director, Dana Edell, and Change.org's women's rights director of organizing, Shelby Knox, talked with Julia and her parents about possible next steps. Meanwhile, the SPARKteam met to consider a creative and fun action to give the petition more visibility, settling on a mock photo shoot outside *Seventeen* headquarters in Manhattan. SPARK and Change.org sent out a series of press releases announcing the photo shoot and petition delivery and flew Julia and her mother to New York City to be part of the action.

The morning of the mock photo shoot, a group of SPARKteam girls met at Change.org's headquarters with Julia and her mom as well as Jamia Wilson, then vice president of programming for the Women's Media Center,[8] Edell, and Knox to prepare their action. The girls decided to wear SPARK Movement tees and carry whiteboard signs with colorful slogans they brainstormed, like TEEN GIRLS AGAINST PHOTOSHOP and THIS MAGAZINE'S FOR ME? MAKE IT LOOK LIKE ME! The group talked strategy and Wilson offered the girls some last-minute media training, advising them about how best to interact with journalists and stay on message.

The photo shoot was inundated with press, and Shoket quickly invited Julia, her mom, and Edell to her office for a cupcake-sweetened chat. Soon after, *Seventeen* published its Body Peace Treaty. The SPARKteam blogged about the events leading up to their public win, even as two other members, Carina and Emma, prepared to launch their own petition to challenge *Teen Vogue* to follow suit.

Make no mistake about it, Julia's passion for the issue, as well as her intelligence and poise in the midst of a flurry of media attention, was all hers. But the effectiveness and reach of her activism, as well as her thoughtful responses to the press, had much to do with the support and preparation she'd received. Her fellow teammates carried her cause forward. Adults working with SPARK challenged her to think deeply and critically about the issues and enabled her to reach far beyond what she could accomplish on her own. Behind the scenes, a well-organized intergenerational partnership strategized with her, offered experience and perspective and financial assistance, and then helped spread the word far and wide. Julia was an experienced, connected, and fully supported fourteen-year-old activist initiating the right action at the right cultural moment with the right tools and platform at her disposal. Does it really matter that the media's version of Julia's success is not an accurate telling? Julia told me why she thinks so.

We got a lot of press for *Seventeen* magazine but they only talked about like half the story. They made it sound like, "Oh this girl from a small town started this petition by herself and got like thousands of signatures." And that's really unrealistic because there was so much more work done behind the scenes by everyone at SPARK and the girls and all of the partner organizations that made it possible. It creates, like, an unrealistic idea that, "Oh, if you start a petition, you can just change the world," but it's a lot, there's a lot more work put into it. So I guess the story of what we are doing needs to be recognized more, but also needs to be recognized correctly; like they need to include everything we did for it and stuff and not just leave out half the story.

Julia became so frustrated with journalists' creative editing, the erasure of layers of support and of her coalition work with Izzy, Maya, and the other girls on the SPARKteam, that she began to accept interviews only when SPARK was "recognized correctly." In one such interview with Laura Zegel at Viral Media Lab,[9] Julia spoke about the connection she saw between the way fashion magazines airbrush images of models and the way journalists edited her story.

I was the one who wrote the petition, but getting 86,000 signatures on it was the work of all of the SPARK movement members, and our 60+ sister organizations. They shared it with everyone they knew, posted it all over the internet, wrote blogs, and Izzy Labbe made a video that received over 13,000 views. Whenever I was interviewed by the press, I always talked a lot about SPARK, but they always ended up cutting that out. That really bothered me.

Photoshop is used in many cases because companies think that if they show perfect girls in their ads, they will make the buyer feel inadequate, and therefore buy the product. I relate that to how the press changed my story, because they also changed the product to make more money. They probably thought the headline starting "One Teenage Girl From Maine . . ." would make more money than the headline starting "A Group of 20 Activist Teens . . . ," so they changed it.

Julia understood both the market value of her story and the heavy costs to girls everywhere of reducing her complex set of experiences to "special girl" status. Telling a "you start a petition, you can change the world" story of individual effort erased the very conditions necessary for the action's success and vital to the education of other girls who might want to become activists like her.[10] Because the media consistently suppressed collective collaboration and instead hyped Julia's individual achievement, she and her team lost a genuine opportunity to educate youth and the adults who work with them about the most important truth about effective social-change work: you don't do it alone.

The Economy of Specialness

In her wonderful biographical collection of social-change makers, *Do It Anyway*, Courtney Martin describes activists as "breathtakingly ordinary."[11] And it's true. Youth activists are in every school and community, doing the hard and messy political work of making their corner of the world a better place. We don't hear much about them because their stories of local resistance and dissent don't usually map on to our version of good girls, good leaders, or even good citizens, especially if they are girls of color or queer girls challenging inhospitable learning environments. Grassroots student activism directed at school policies that address sexual harassment, racial bias, or school suspension rates are unlikely to make it into the local paper unless discipline is involved.

The girl activists whose stories make the nightly news are the ones easily reimagined into salable commodities. Arranging these accounts for mass consumption is not unlike staging a home for sale: one attracts the greatest pool of prospective buyers to a property by getting rid of the clutter, removing signs of relationships, family stories, cultural background, lived experience—anything that might prevent people from seeing themselves in the space. Julia's experiences, rich with personal history, economic and racial privilege, parental availability, adult support, and organizational training had to be cleared out. Elements unique to her that had made a difference in her life were removed; any fears and anxieties and failures she might have had were swept under the rug. We are left with the most widely appealing (marketable) version of her story, a default option for the masses: a young, special everygirl.

In a media culture where journalists both hype and wring their hands over the current state of (too aggressive, too slutty, too mouthy, too bitchy) girlhood, the perfect sale is the fantasized feminine ideal, unmarked by race or class or sexuality, unmarred by localized identities or experiences. A salable story has a combination of youthful innocence and precocious entrepreneurial independence in the form of what political and social inquiry professor Anita Harris calls the "can-do" girl—ambitious, self-reliant, in control.[12] Thirteen-year-old McKenna Pope's story works on all counts. McKenna petitioned toy-maker Hasbro for a gender-neutral Easy-Bake oven for her budding chef of a little brother. The commodified version of McKenna's story pits a sweet, determined eighth grader against a major toy company, the love of a little brother against corporate profit. We don't know who advised McKenna, who taught her how to write an effective petition or get it to the desk of Hasbro's CEO, or even who paid for all those printed petitions she handed over or her travel costs to Hasbro's headquarters. If we did, McKenna would be, well, a bit less extraordinary.

When high schoolers Emma Axelrod, Elena Tsemberis, and Sammi Siegel learned that the last woman to moderate a presidential debate was Carole Simpson in 1992, they wrote a petition asking the Commission on Presidential Debates to name a woman moderator in 2012. This story, too, went viral. The fact that the girls attended an elite program at their high school, the Civics and Government Institute, where they learned about social movements from a social studies teacher who took special interest in their cause,[13] the fact that their privilege ensured that attention, invested energy, and public accolades would flow in their direction is just not news. If they're not exceptional (i.e., do-it-yourselfers) there's no story.

Petitions fit nicely within the economy of the special girl. They throw young activists into sharp relief. Smiling can-do girls delivering large boxes of petitions to a popular magazine or corporate headquarters makes for a great photo op. And ironically, once the background details are cropped out, once the complexity and reality of girls' lives are stripped away, they become blank screens onto which we can project our hopes and dreams for all girls. They give us reason to believe in a system that rewards self-reliance and the illusion that the deserving just worked a little harder. Ironic, of course, because cropping out these details makes it unlikely such dreams will be realized.

These public stories of specialness are enabled by what University of California–Davis design professor Simon Sadler calls the current "TEDification of thought and discourse." TED talks by young activists tend to convey what Sadler summarizes as a "Pollyanna-ish optimism," a "big picture" focus, and an "exception is the rule" philosophy. In "TED World," thinkers and actors "are not so much exceptional figures as *models* from which we can abstract the rules of innovation." In other words, "everyone can rise out of poverty and adversity, since we know that *some* rise out of poverty and adversity."[14] Every girl can have an impact on corporate policy because one girl did.

TED speakers are coached to tell their stories in much the same way realty clients are coached to stage their houses. When Julia Bluhm and Izzy Labbe were preparing their TEDWomen talk about SPARK's *Seventeen* action, for example, they were advised to tell *their* story, meaning the "special girl" story, apart from the intergenerational movement that educated and supported them. Only in what Sadler calls the "magical thinking" realm of TED talks is it possible to separate the multiple layers of support involved in an action and the success of that action.

McKenna was likely coached too, since she tells her Easy-Bake oven story at TEDYouth 2013 in this "can do" way: "I'm McKenna Pope and when I was 13, I convinced one of the largest toy companies in the world, Hasbro, to change the way they marketed one of their best-selling products." McKenna does, indeed, deliver a "rousing call to action to all kids who feel powerless," assuring her young listeners that "your voice matters" and advising them to "make your change. I know you can. . . . You can take what you believe in and turn it into a cause . . . and you can use that spark that you have within you and turn it into a fire."[15]

So does Emma Axelrod, who in her TED talk tells her audience to just "think of something that you would like to change and think of how you can do it, and I guarantee you that if it is a cause worth changing your community will back you up and they will help you."[16] So does Maya Penn, at thirteen already a gifted young activist, artist, techie, designer, and entrepreneur: "Ideas can spark a movement. Ideas are opportunities and innovation. Ideas truly are what make the world go round. At eight years old, I took my ideas and started my own business called Maya's Ideas, and my nonprofit, Maya's Ideas for the Planet."[17]

A big yes to creativity, passion, and initiative; a bigger yes to girls' agency and self-confidence. But it matters that Maya is the daughter of an artist and successful entrepreneur, that she's home-schooled and has access to all the technology, information, and resources she could possibly need to be her best creative self. What are the hundreds of kids in the room and the thousands watching McKenna, Emma, and Maya online supposed to *do* exactly? They, too, may have a keen eye for injustice, a dream, a passion for making the world a better place, wonderful and creative ideas, but how do they get from here to there without guideposts, without the conditions necessary to create social change?

These TED talks, like the mainstream media stories that inspire them, sit firmly within the pocket of "can-do" girlhood, and function, gender studies professor and activist Emily Bent explains, "as regulatory illusions, making the ideals of autonomy and choice seem not only plausible but also desirable."[18] They use appealing young girls to perpetuate the myth that all we need is passion, individual effort, and a sassy assertiveness to create the world we want.[19]

In reality, of course, not all voices matter or matter in the same way. Journalists, marketers, and TED organizers who know the value of "seeming not to be anything in particular," as George Lipsitz says in his book *The Possessive Investment in Whiteness*, decided these were stories worth staging and sharing.[20] The exception, of course, is not the rule. The exception is the exception made possible by layers of privilege and support. In truth, most girls don't know how to initiate an action that addresses the daily indignities they witness or experience. Most don't have who and what they need. Few go to specialized "learning communities" that nurture their activist tendencies or have teachers or parents who notice and take their dissent seriously. Few girls live in communities that will back them up, regardless of how much passion they have or how worthy their cause. For those who don't, such a well-intentioned call to action has the opposite of its intended effect. When stories are staged and narratives stripped of the scaffolding that ensured their success, they inadvertently shore up privilege and set up all but a special few for a sense of helplessness, failure, and judgment.

A special girl can inspire, but she's barely left the stage before reality sets in. Returning home to peers and adults who don't get it, to an underresourced community, to a school with a scarcity of clubs and organizations, a family that needs her to help care for siblings, or parents who hold her close and monitor her whereabouts or simply want her to fit in rather than stand out, can dampen the most passionate inner fire. Such realities set up barriers to a girl's civic participation, constrain her options, and make it a lot harder for her to engage in public dissent about the injustices she sees.[21]

Special Girl or Shill?

Contemporary girls have grown up with reality shows, nighttime soaps, PG-13 movies, and seemingly endless chick-lit book series in which the sum of a girl's worth is a good makeover and a coveted job in fashion design. This highly profitable consumer version of Girl Power casts freedom and choice as purchasing power and privilege as individual achievement, diverting attention away from community and political engagement.[22] Girls have always pushed back in creative ways, refusing to be contained, interrupting and disrupting the whitewashing of lived experience, underscoring what Nigerian novelist Chimamanda Ngozi Adichie calls "the danger of a single story."[23] But they are up against a formidable juggernaut of consumer culture that seeks to control the narrative. Julia Bluhm learned this firsthand. Not just journalists, but foundations, schools, community centers, even feminist organizations wanted the story of her activism to be just about her.

In her examination of the Girl Effect, a stunningly successful campaign initiated by the Nike Foundation to raise money for girls' education in the Global South, Emily Bent unpacks neoliberal rhetoric that suggests girls can lead themselves, without support, "through a series of never-ending achievements." "Girls are the most powerful force for change on the planet," the Nike Foundation asserts. Invest in a girl and "she will do the rest."[24] Bent calculates the costs of "rendering invisible and unnecessary girls' familial, geopolitical, and sociocultural support systems" and "dismissing the role of gender inequality, structural difference, and power in their everyday lives and their communities."[25] Establishing an entire global campaign on the absurd notion that "girls are only successful when they are completely and utterly alone,"[26] she argues, defies all logic. It defies everything we know about how effective social change happens.

In the neoliberal economy of specialness, in fact, any mention of adult or community support kicks in another opposing narrative. A girl who's not exceptional enough to negotiate a series of never-ending achievements is worse than ordinary; she's a front for adult causes. This is a zero-sum game. She can't win for losing—either she does something remarkable all on her own, which ignores social reality, or she is a pawn, easily used or manipulated and worthy of dismissal.

At fourteen, Rachel Parent, clad in a white T-shirt and jeans, a protest sign tucked under her arm, stood in front of a microphone at a public rally and called out Kevin O'Leary, the Canadian venture capitalist and broadcast personality known as "Mr. Wonderful" to viewers of ABC's reality show *Shark Tank*, for condemning protesters seeking to halt agribusinesses from using genetically modified organisms (GMOs) in crop production.

> I want to respond to Mr. Kevin O'Leary's idiotic statement about "stupid people's" protest against Monsanto. While on the *Lang and O'Leary* show, which aired on CBC May twenty-seventh, Kevin O'Leary said to all of us, and I quote, "I have an answer to these people. Stop eating; then we can get rid of them." Well, I challenge you, Mr. O'Leary, to have me on your show next week, and if you promise not to use the word *stupid*, then I won't use the word *fascist*.[27]

Rachel was quickly invited onto the show, where she fielded persistent challenges to her credibility and her authenticity. By nearly all accounts, she won the debate with her clear grasp of the scientific evidence, but not before O'Leary did what so many adults do with seasoned girl activists—he accused her of being a "shill" for environmental organizations: "You're very articulate, that's a positive; what I'm concerned about and what I'm exploring with you is whether you've become a shill for a group that wants to use you because you're young, you're articulate, you're getting lots of media, and I'm happy for you on that. But I'm trying to figure out whether you really deep down believe this."

Of course Rachel has had lots of adult support over the course of her activist campaigns. Of course she's been educated by those within the anti-GMO movement. A girl of twelve cannot organize an activist campaign all alone—no one person of any age can. We all need help navigating the system and making things happen. But how are Rachel Parent and other girl activists supposed to respond to the likes of Kevin O'Leary? What can they say when any support from adults suggests they cannot possibly be smart enough, strong enough, brave enough, passionate enough to engage effectively in social-change work? Within the framework offered, the pressure is on to affirm their autonomy and specialness. And the pressure is on for those of us who support girl activists to lie low.

If anyone is using girl activists for profit, of course, it's the Kevin O'Learys of the world. Corporations and foundations routinely invoke girls like Pakistani activist Malala Yousafzai, Rachel Parent, and Julia Bluhm as carefully crafted examples of neoliberal Girl Power in campaigns to raise millions for the education of girls in the Global South. "Girls are increasingly being publicly celebrated as community leaders, models of ideal citizenship, and central to economic development," sociologist Jessica Taft argues. But "what kinds of political and civic engagement practices are celebrated by such narratives and what kinds are excluded?"[28]

Again, what's conveniently excluded are the relational and material conditions vital to sustaining genuine activist work—the kind of work that challenges and threatens the way things typically go. Intergenerational activism is anathema to the salable narrative of the special girl because it troubles the girl/adult binary. Moreover, activism demands critical thinking, and critical thinking has no popular appeal in the marketplace because it incites discontent with the status quo. We begin to see, as cultural critic Henry Giroux says, the neoliberal occupations of our imaginations,[29] how the endless creativity of the social sphere is subjected to market-driven machinations, resulting in disembedded individuals spouting such commercial clichés as "I did it, and with enough passion, determination, and self-confidence you can too!" But imagination, Maxine Greene says, "is inherently relational. It's what enables us to cross the empty spaces . . . to give credence to alternative realities. It allows us to break with the taken for granted, to set aside familiar distinctions and definitions."[30]

In reality, most US girls have little access even to the most basic understanding of social-change work. When Jessica Taft interviewed girl activists from five different countries across the Americas, she discovered that those from the United States were less likely to identify themselves as activists or even to know what the word *activism* meant. Youth from the other countries in her study—Argentina, Venezuela, Mexico, and Canada—had a richer vocabulary and set of experiences to draw from. They were more likely to work within intergenerational movements and to know the history of activism in their communities and countries—fertile ground, Taft explains, for a politics of learning, participation, and hope. Interestingly, the girl activists Taft interviewed, those doing the work as part of their everyday lives, "adamantly and actively refute the idea that they are special." For those engaged in the work, activism is "an ordinary practice."[31]

As I write this, the feminist blogosphere is on fire with the creation of the Radical Brownies, now the Radical Monarchs, an Oakland, California, troop of girls ages eight to twelve that "empowers young girls of color to step into their collective power, brilliance and leadership to make the world a more radical place." Unaffiliated with the Girl Scouts of America, the Radical Monarchs earn badges for their involvement in activism: "Black Lives Matter," "LGBT Ally," and "Food Justice," for example. As one blogger writes, "Why sell thin mints when you could be starting a revolution?"[32]

It is unsurprising that the group has not made national news— at least outside feminist outlets. The Radical Monarchs don't fit the "special girl" story. They are not containable within the usual can-do narrative. They are community-based, collective, and un-apologetically intergenerational and intersectional. In a videotaped chat on the Radical Monarch's Facebook page, cofounders Marilyn Hollinquest and Anayvette Martinez, both well versed in youth development and community activism, tell a rich story of organic beginnings. Informed by their own experiences growing up as girls of color, they want girls in their community to have what they didn't—opportunities for "trans and gender-nonconforming inclusive spaces," where they can "embrace the spectrum of gender diversity," know their histories of resistance, experience support from adults who respect their contributions, and "form bonds of sisterhood with other girls."[33] Hollinquest and Martinez are under no illusion that eight-year-old girls can do social justice work without experienced adult support and community engagement. They are also firm in their belief that the girls they work with are experts on their own experiences and quite capable of girl-fueled activist projects.

The Radical Monarchs are not inspired by "special girl" stories. Rather, their inspiration comes in the form of two adult women the girls know well and the history of social movements these women impart, "movements grown by the community . . . that fight for justice for their communities." The only way such a diverse and radical intergenerational group of activists might attract the attention of mainstream media like the *New York Times* is if the Girl Scouts of America threaten them with copyright infringement. And the reaction they've received from other venues outside feminist media thus far has been predictable: "Is this a welcome riff off of scouting or a disturbing radicalization of young children?" one blogger asks.[34]

The ordinary practice of intergenerational activism interrupts the narrative of the exceptional girl. In reality, social change is a collective enterprise. We need one another; our work and our play are about struggling together to find solutions to the problems in front of us. Girls and young women are a powerful force when they protest inequality and oppression in their everyday lives—when they address homophobia in their school hallways, street harassment in their neighborhoods, online racist and sexist comments and threats.

Our role as adults is to create the conditions for these conversations, to render visible necessary support systems, to use our power to move solutions forward, and to ensure that we do as we say—over and over and over again so that we produce the effect that we name.[35] This is how girls come to know and trust us, how they begin to authorize themselves as activists with the right to claim social reality and make history.[36] This is how effective change happens—grounded in the complexity of lived experience and dependent on relationships, reliant on histories of resistance, secured, repeated, and practiced. This is how we induce hopefulness. And hope, of course, is not a commodity but something we create together. Hope lives in the messy possibilities relationships offer. It's fed by small daily successes to local problems and it's sustained by youthful optimism.

CHAPTER TWO

Everyday Rebellions

Recently I was asked to consult on a new leadership program for high school girls, funded by a wealthy businesswoman. According to the planning documents I received, the program was designed to help girls discover their "inner compass," learn to take personal responsibility for their actions, develop networking skills and social media manners. The goal was to prepare girls to enter the world with "grit" and "a personal brand." The businesswoman—"her story, experiences, successes, and international recognition"— would anchor a series of daylong training sessions, and over the course of the year other "successful women leaders" would model key concepts and offer information to the girls. There would be time and opportunity for the girls to ask these women questions, and the girls would even be invited to emcee a panel of professional women and politicians.

I encouraged the program director to rethink this approach, to consider opportunities for the women and girls to learn from one another, perhaps inviting the girls to identify a meaningful problem and to work with the women to plan a solution. I stressed the importance of building deeper intergenerational relationships and the advantages of creating something original together. I advocated a move away from a focus on girls' self-improvement and dependence on women's expertise and toward women and girls engaging one another, sharing knowledge, and critiquing and challenging unfair systems and practices together. After a series of meetings and emails, we amicably agreed to part ways.

In my experience, those who work with girls often get anxious when I suggest we talk about igniting girl-fueled activism. Instead they want to talk about preparing girls for leadership. For a time, this confused me. I didn't draw clear distinctions between the two. Participating in activism offers an opportunity to identify a problem, work in coalition, leverage allies and energize people, think critically, listen well, speak up, stand up, and take calculated risks—all leadership skills.

But after a series of conversations like the one described above, I've come to understand that the differences between leadership—at least as it's often practiced today in relation to girls—and activism have everything to do with locus of control. *Girls leadership program* is typically code for teaching girls how to fit in, how to "lean in," to "get a seat at the table."[1] Such "normative" civic and political engagement programs, Jessica Taft argues, assume a world full of danger, and measure personal success as the ability to navigate or overcome obstacles that derive from taken-for-granted systems.[2] Our role as adults is to model the skills that have worked for those few at the top and to supervise girls' assimilation into the current system.

Activist work, on the other hand, is an invitation to engage in critical analysis of the systems girls interact with, and, Taft says, to "imagine the public sphere as a space they can shape."[3] Engaging in such "transformative" work with girls is an admission by women that we've botched some things and that they may be in a position to do better. Our adult responsibility is not to model individual strategies, not to create "Mini-Me's," but to work collaboratively with girls in ways that enable their best thinking, that activate their imaginations. We have an ethical responsibility, Emily Bent argues, "to alter institutional barriers and obstacles that threaten all girls as empowered political subjects."[4] And so we participate with girls in order "for all of us to feel that this is our world,"[5] in the words of Bernice Johnson Reagon, activist and founder of the musical collective Sweet Honey in the Rock.

While I'll never quite understand how girls learn to lead without actually leading, without the power and the opportunity to fully participate in and struggle with what matters from the ground up and without learning firsthand how "to push, shove, and elbow their ways into the democratic process,"[6] I do understand why girl-fueled activism can be anxiety-producing, even for those who value transformative approaches. It suggests disruption. Inviting girls to identify an injustice and develop a plan to address it seems like inviting trouble, opening a door to the unruly, something already associated with adolescence, and inviting drama, something already associated with girls. Inviting girls to closely examine and actively question what we've taken for granted as good and fair can leave us feeling groundless, unstable. It all starts to sound like an accident waiting to happen. Leadership, on the other hand, suggests order, predictability, professionalism; it's something that mature adults have and youth need to learn. Offering our hard-earned wisdom and experience in the form of thoughtfully constructed presentations and training or well-vetted service learning and civic-engagement projects ensures that girls today develop the skills they need to become leaders tomorrow.

But let me trouble the smooth waters of leadership training and make a case for a little activist splashing around. The well-documented pressure so many girls feel in early adolescence to dismiss what's most real and important to them in order to be validated and taken seriously comes largely from the conditions we, as adults, have created.[7] Plugging girls into prefabricated systems and encouraging them to succeed on someone else's terms fails to give them what they need most: practice developing their own ideas, trusting their own experiences and perspectives, building connections with peers and relationships with adults that make it possible to stay present and whole even as—especially as—they risk dissent. No predesigned leadership experience—even one that offers girls some measure of choice or agency—can replace the power and creative skill required to develop an idea in coalition with others, tackle a personally meaningful problem, and participate in creating solutions that feel good and right. No program for future leaders or exposure to advice-offering experts can come close to the benefits of organizing for a cause right here, right now. Activism is experientially grounded leadership training and absolutely necessary for a politics built on passionate belief. Activism is all about relationship building, working across differences and through disagreements, finding common ground, acting, and then taking care of one another when things don't go as planned. When girls do activism, individual leaders can emerge, but typically they pop up organically, tied to issues they feel passionate about, in response to problems that require their special skills, and in relationship with others who share the wider goals of the project. This form of leadership is more horizontal as girls link "their identities as girls and their organizational practices" with an emphasis on "listening, building relationships, sharing power, caring about other people."[8]

Girl-fueled and girl-led activism has everything to do with girls' experiences of ownership, authorship, and control over their lives, so vital to their healthy development. Adults who offer girls what they need to figure out what they stand for—the space and opportunity to think critically with others about the world around them—affirm for girls the power of their own minds and hearts. And girls who are encouraged to see beneath the surface of things—whether it's the feel-good glitz of media advertising, the false promises and dangers of a pull-yourself-up-by-your-bootstraps meritocracy, or straight-faced justification for policies laced and layered with sexism, racism, and homophobia—are psychologically healthier and more confident.[9] Adults who value what girls bring to a process, who pose genuine questions, point out contradictions, and create safe spaces for honest reflection and discussion, offer girls what they need to hone and practice skills so vital to both personal development and political citizenship. This kind of talk is not cheap. There is nothing more revitalizing and powerful than tackling an issue you really understand and feel personally invested in with others you trust to accompany and support you.

Every girl has the potential to be an agent for social change in her school or community, simply because, as bell hooks reminds us, children are naturally curious and "organically predisposed to be critical thinkers."[10] This tendency to be naturalists in the social world—to observe, wonder, and question—is at the heart of healthy resistance to unfairness and hurt;[11] it's fundamental to what clinician Annie Rogers means when she defines courage as the ability "to speak one's mind by telling all one's heart."[12]

The energy and curiosity, the gender-bending border-crossing physicality, intensity, and irreverence we can so welcome and enjoy in children, however, is too often cause for concern and wariness in adolescence. We change in response to girls' changes; as they grow up we often see their curiosity as impertinence, their astute observations about the way the world works as a challenge. As our control wanes, what they feel and think about us gains traction and threatens to take hold, to become larger than us, to become political. "No longer is it merely for the old to teach the young the meaning of life," psychologist Erik Erikson once wrote of adolescence. "It is the young who, by their responses and actions, tell the old whether life as represented to them has some vital promise, and it is the young who carry in them the power to confirm those who confirm them, to renew and regenerate, to disavow what is rotten, to reform and rebel."[13] The protective walls we throw up and guard are destined to come down.

Moving Beyond Fear and Good Intentions

African American studies and performance professor Aimee Meredith Cox argues that "research on adolescence has largely been written from the perspective of fear," and so perhaps unsurprisingly, "control and containment is a recurring theme,"[14] especially in practice. Cox asks us to take seriously not just our generational fear of becoming irrelevant, but our anxieties when the developmental ideals we hold on to—what we think it means to be an adolescent, what we think it means to be a girl—are threatened by the complex lived realities of the girls we work with. Can we resist our impulse to judge and contain those who challenge us? Can we use our authority and power to make it easier for girls to speak and be heard, to encourage political resistance, even when—perhaps especially when—the truths girls speak and the actions they pursue lead us to places we're afraid to go?

In her ethnography of black women in a Detroit homeless shelter, Cox describes "the thick, complex, richly textured, and uncategorizable aspects of the lives of low-income Black women" and how they "shapeshift" in the face of dehumanizing discourses, labels, and assumptions "hurled at them from multiple points of origin."[15] Being in relationship with women who have lived experiences so different from her own requires Cox to make an effort to know what one of the shelter residents describes as the "missing middle"—to move beyond assumptions and expectations to see the complex truth of the women she works with, "their legibility as fully human."[16] The possibility of relationship for Cox, for all of us, begins when we can critically explore and confront what prevents our view of the missing middle. Ironically, what gets in our way is not fully visible until we begin our work together. And we fear what we do not know, what we cannot see.

If containment, control, and discipline are reactions to such fear, then, judging by the public surveillance and shaming girls so often receive, many of us are very afraid indeed. In the face of girls' rich and complex lives situated in shifting and precarious social contexts, their insistence on not being one thing or another makes sense. Resistance to pressures and expectations that they pass inspection—that they perform a physically controlled and compliant version of a girl who talks right, acts right, looks right, and dresses a particular way—is a sign girls take themselves seriously. Given the impact of visual media to repeat and normalize a narrow version of femininity, one that imbues social power to those who are thin, light-skinned, able-bodied, pleasing and appealing to boys, resistance is a sign of health, not risk. It's our response that makes girls' resistance risky.

Assimilating to such ideals isn't good for girls; it undermines girls' connections to their families and communities, threatens their curiosity and their tendency to question what doesn't feel good or seem quite right. It's especially troublesome and damaging when a narrow version of femininity is pressed on girls in schools. In the early 1990s anthropologist Signithia Fordham, for example, delineated the disconnect high-achieving black girls too often experience between their home culture and school, where they are under pressure from teachers to be a particular kind of girl, expected "to perform all assigned tasks while remaining silent, to respond as if absent rather than present." Their school achievement came at the expense of their own voices.[17] And those "loud, Black girls" who refused to participate in [their] own exclusion paid a different kind of educational price. They were tagged "low-achievers" and troublemakers.

This pattern has held over time. Over a decade later, sociologist Edward Morris observed the ways teachers disciplined high-achieving black girls who don't conform to "lady-like" behaviors, such as passivity, deference, and bodily control. The girls' "loud and confrontational behavior" was "viewed as a defect that compromised their very femininity," and so their teachers doled out admonitions and instructions designed "to mold them" into becoming more acceptably feminine, which meant "being quieter and more passive." Their teachers' surveillance, Morris concluded, came at the expense of the girls' curiosity, outspokenness, and assertiveness—the very qualities a good teacher dreams about.[18]

A version of this discipline and pressure to act feminine in white middle-class ways extends to poor and working-class white girls I've listened to. Girls express anger and frustration at their teachers' excessive interest in the way they speak and present themselves. Teachers can impart a sense of shame and inadequacy, of failing to fit in or match up that has nothing to do with the girls' intellectual capabilities, but of course affects their engagement in school and their confidence in their school performance.[19] The girls' boisterous interactions, direct expression of their thoughts and feelings, and tendency to take up space in physically playful ways are interpreted as improper and excessive. In response, the girls think of themselves as "stupid" for not knowing what adults want and complain bitterly about their teachers' power to judge and punish them when they haven't made the effort to see the "missing middle." School, for so many girls, is complicated and confusing terrain, a place where they feel unrecognizable, dismissed, shamed, and out of sync.

It's seductive to think that simply caring for girls will keep us from making judgments and punishments. But those disciplining girls' behavior and bodies in these studies include well-intentioned women teachers fully invested in the success of girls in their charge. In Morris's study, the teachers more likely to control and castigate black girls for their lack of middle-class social skills and unladylike behavior were black women teachers who hoped to prepare and protect girls from the inevitable racism coming their way. The women teachers most concerned with correcting the poor white and working-class girls were those who grew up in the same impoverished community, wishing to inculcate behaviors associated with academic success. These things aren't simple. To some degree, we are all implicated.

Which means we share responsibility. When critique, open dissent, and genuine curiosity, necessary for both high achievement and activist identities, are deemed unfeminine and undisciplined, girls spend an inordinate amount of energy trying to read adults and the social environment, improvising ways to enact their anger, confusion, and frustration, creatively challenging authority, testing limits, or simply refusing to go along with what they experience as unfair and hurtful. In the raucous presence of such girls, it's difficult to appreciate the importance of what they are doing, the possibilities right in front of us, the potential of such energy if it could be fully embraced, engaged, freed up, and channeled into meaningful activism and political participation.

Transformative organizations enable girls to think critically about systemic injustices and teach them how to make social change in their schools and communities. In Girls for Gender Equity (GGE) in New York City, for example, fifteen young women of color worked together for two years as Sisters in Strength (SIS) youth organizers to tackle hostile school environments. Well aware of recent reports affirming what they know from experience— that black girls receive much harsher discipline than their white peers—SIS organizers collected essays, poems, and art from young women of color that illustrate how it feels to be seen as dangerous, to experience hostility from teachers, to have their self-expression and movements curtailed.

I attended a presentation of the SIS research entitled "Dangerous Bodies: Girls of Color and Harsh Discipline," and the results were moving and deeply troubling.[20] WELCOME FRIENDS, ALLIES, AND LEARNERS, their brightly colored poster announced, inviting us in to their presentation of the "missing middle." WE ARE STILL HUMANKIND. WE CAN STILL FEEL. We viewed a video the young women made about the kinds of indignities they experience daily. We took a "gallery walk" of their stories and art, which reminded us over and over again what racism looks like and how it feels to be seen as dangerous, to be treated as a problem. We read, saw, and heard the emotional, psychological, and academic costs of going to school every day under a cloud of suspicion and surveillance.

As adults, we can see girls' noncompliance as signs of impudence or threat to sanctioned versions of school and society or we can see *them*, hear *them*, center *them*. The former option is easier, but we must know that this choice, regardless of our good intentions, risks psychological suffering and political trouble. Choosing the latter means choosing relationship, choosing opportunities, envisioning alternatives that affirm girls' experiences and social realities.[21] Girls and young women who refuse to camouflage their thoughts and feelings, who are willing to speak uncomfortable

truths or question what they see as unfairness and hurtful behaviors, tend to have adult women in their lives—either staff in
transformative organizations like Girls for Gender Equity or, less
formally, parents and "other mothers" of various kinds, such as
neighbors, teachers, ed techs, kitchen cafeteria workers—who
stand with girls and risk being, in poet Adrienne Rich's words, a
"witness in [their] defense."[22] These are adults who invite them in,
listen, and advise them to be loyal to themselves, to be brave and
strong, to speak up about their experiences and act up for what
they believe in.

It's difficult to appreciate while in the midst of a power
struggle with a girl that signs of her resistance, whether open or
"c/overt"[23]—are signs of possibility. Adults who can stay present
in the midst of girls' anger and confusion and sustain open conversation, so vital to political engagement, are lifelines. Girls who
grow up in the midst of such clarity, who do not learn that anger,
dissent, and critical thinking are dangerous, who are encouraged
to refuse "a world that seeks to educate them for conformity and
obedience" are, quite simply, psychologically healthier.[24] And they
have the energy and the support to extend the possibility of this
health and well-being to other girls.

The problem, then, is not the girls, but the conditions we as
adults create, the pressures we exert, the separations we orchestrate,
the walls we construct. We can choose differently, create a new set
of conditions, but only in relationship with girls. The onus is on
us to listen and remain open to the signs of reactive life all around
us, to recognize the various strategies, healthy and unhealthy, girls
use to remain connected and whole in environments that require
them to lop off parts of themselves in order to fit the version of girl
that others seem to want. That version of girl is defined by accommodation to conditions that require her to curtail her creativity
and withhold her voice, that render inappropriate or excessive her
lucid anger at injustice and hurt. Within a set of conditions not of
her making, it's a liability and a transgression for her to assert the
knowledge and contributions derived from her differences.

Our job as adults is to understand what incites dissent and everyday rebellions, *especially* when it bothers us, and to cultivate an ability to step toward such forceful reactions, to interrupt silence, to read the "hidden transcripts" of a girl's resistance[25]—the ways she refigures her protest to be heard through indirect or relational aggression toward other girls, inside jokes, fraudulent niceness, false public agreement, or feigned ignorance when outward dissent would be dismissed, punished, or shamed. Our job is to create safe and legitimate spaces for her to speak her thoughts and feelings, to exercise her imagination, to allow her, in spoken word poet and activist Andrea Gibson's words, to "thaw outside the lines."[26]

This is hard work. A girl's refusal and resistance conjures up our own girlhoods; the trouble we invited, those times when our dissent was quelled through shaming and discipline. When an eleven-year-old girl tells a researcher that she's "terrified" to speak up because things will "turn out to be a mess,"[27] a lot of women know what she means. Publicly supporting girls who put themselves on the line in spite of the mess they might create exposes a set of uneasy compromises we have made, and incites what Judith Butler calls the threat of "uninhabitable identification," an uncomfortable-in-our skin struggle between listening to girls and becoming activated, even politicized, by them, or molding them to our likeness both to shore up our own authority and for their own protection.[28]

In truth, the systems within which we work, if we want to keep working in them, demand a certain allegiance. Girls who question the way things go make us uneasy not only because they remind us of the parts of ourselves we let go, hid, or left behind, but because girls are right: they *are* treated badly, some more so than others, and pushing back *can* make a mess, *can* put things in motion in a way she/we might not be able to stop. It's safer to justify those losses than to revisit them, easier to align with the powers that be—to see disruptive girls as the problem. Easier to let unfair systems and the adults who support them off the hook. It's amazing to me how often guidance counselors I interact with in schools, good people committed to their good work, so easily and quickly label individual girls "mean" or "slutty" or call groups of girls names like "the tough cookies" or "the dirty dozen,"[29] forgetting the complexities of their own lives as girls and the times they balanced precariously on the edge of whatever labels or stereotypes circulated in their schools and communities growing up.

We were no different as girls. We scrambled to secure safe ground, we felt the pleasure and the exposure of speaking our thoughts and feelings; we experienced the collateral damage when other girls risked too much; we targeted one another to prove our comparative goodness or toughness; we hurt and we were hurt, and we talked about all of it with the people we trusted. Why do we expect more from girls than we could give? Why do we expect them to fit within systems that once squeezed the life out of us?

In her article "Joining the Resistance: Psychology, Politics, Girls, and Women," Carol Gilligan lists five psychological truths. The second is this: "The hallmarks of loss are idealization and rage, and under the rage, immense sadness. ('To want and want and not to have.')"[30] There is a pernicious pattern of loss that props up the idealization we impose on girls. We know the deeply complicated entanglements, the intricate system of exclusive ins and outs, the injustices and cruelties tied by invisible threads to power and privilege. It helps to explain why even those of us who facilitate girls empowerment groups, who believe we are cultivating girls' voices, unwittingly suppress their interruptions, silence their angry questions, ignore their whispered protests, and step away from the contradictions they expose.[31] It's difficult to listen and respond to experiences that pull us back to the desires and truths we ourselves once struggled with, were judged by, and punished for.

Choosing Girls

"When I advocate for the most vulnerable girls and women at the intersection of gender, race, class, and sexual oppression," Girls for Gender Equity founder and director Joanne Smith says, "I'm advocating for myself and my family."[32] Effectively working with girls requires us to look at our work through the lens of our most difficult and painful experiences—the times when we were not listened to, taken seriously, excluded; when systemic inequities and the abuse of adult power and privilege cost us the full complexity of what we could offer and demanded that we betray people we loved or let go of communities that nurtured us. This reflexivity, this search for increasing complexity, is what it means to stand with girls. From this humble vantage point, we are more able to see them, more able to pay attention to what's happening in the moment. As we become open to and honest about the realities that challenge and decenter us, our relationships with girls shift and we can begin, as Butler says, "hearing beyond what we are able to hear."[33]

Amy Sullivan, Harvard Medical School associate director of education research, refers to such intimate, generative connections with girls as muse relationships—relationships in which "girls can speak freely" and women "share their own experiences" as they "listen to, understand, and validate girls' feeling and experiences."[34] Muse relationships, Sullivan argues, are not only vital to girls' health and well-being, but hold "the potential for developing a critical consciousness that can inspire challenges to oppressive social structures and conventions that silence girls and women."[35] In other words, developing such "evocative" relationships between girls and women is deeply political work.

In the service of creating empowering connections with adolescent girls, hip-hop activist and gender studies professor Ruth Nicole Brown distinguishes between reinforcement and reflective mechanisms. Mechanisms of reinforcement, she explains, maintain the status quo and, because they "inspire borders that are not dissolved, crossed, or negotiated," lead to disconnection." Reflective mechanisms, on the other hand, "deconstruct the mythology of the border. The connections inspired as a result are generative; creating an intimacy that affirms the volunteer's practice and symbolizes political resistance in a culture that has arguably no language to describe connections between women and girls."[36]

Reflection or reinforcement. Those of us who raise, teach, and work with girls make tough choices all the time about how we will react to girls in our charge. Negotiating the boundaries of intergenerational activism is relationally messy, Emily Bent says, and more often than not we're making it up as we go.[37] It's important to remember, however, as psychologist Janie Victoria Ward underscores in her study of African American families,[38] there is a connection between the messages girls receive about how to relate to the worlds they live in and the resistance strategies they use. Girls who are disciplined or punished for their failure to conform or assimilate to untenable or unjust conditions are likely to seek short-term individual solutions as a way to cope and get by. Ward calls these "resistance for survival" strategies—quick fixes to frustration, rage, fear, and disillusionment, such as fighting, walking away, and taking risks that assuage their immediate pain and frustration but do little to change the situation for the better. Such resistance strategies may be self-defeating in the long run, but in the moment they are understandable responses to feeling misunderstood, hurt, or treated badly; they offer a sense of personal control over unbearable or unfair conditions.

If we see behavior as "not simply pathological or pro-social, but rather 'probable' given the toxic context in which behavior occurs," educator-activist Sean Ginwright argues, "it leaves room for agency and highlights the various choices that young people make in their social settings."[39] We begin to see youth responses as understandable, rational reactions to unfairness and hurt, and we begin to see how we, as adults, can do more to positively influence the probable. This does not mean youth are not accountable for their behaviors. It does mean their choices are encumbered, selected from a limited range of options, often within stressful or hostile conditions they have little control over. Influencing the probable directs us toward intergenerational activism. What conditions make students believe this was the only or best choice? How can we work together to alter these conditions? These are questions that move us toward change, toward social transformation.

We are accountable, then, not for fixing girls and young women, but for providing them with opportunities to understand, engage with, and potentially transform what limits and harms them. Providing a girl with what she needs to persist in the face of oppression means connecting her with opportunities to be a catalyst, to participate in the transformation of her environment. Adults willing to stand with girls, affirm their realities, and enable them to think critically provide the conditions for what Ward calls "resistance for liberation." We offer a wider perspective and deeper, more critical awareness about how the world works, which opens the door to possibilities for long-term solutions. The shift to activism is natural, offering girls spaces where they can feel whole, think clearly, and practice dissent and bravery when their sense of integrity is threatened. Girls with such support are more likely to identify and understand problems and work together with adults to formulate ideas and imagine new possibilities.

CHAPTER THREE

Activism Is Good for (All) Girls

I ran my first Girls Coalition Group in a local junior high school with three of my undergraduate students, including Megan Williams and Jackie Dupont, who would, in time, become the first hired staff at Hardy Girls Healthy Women, a transformative girl-serving nonprofit I cofounded in 2000. Inspired by "hardiness" research, which suggests that when people are under stress, they need more control in their lives, more commitment from others, and more challenge or opportunities to be catalysts in their environments, we imagined "hardiness zones" as intergenerational spaces that foster critical thinking and enable girls to transform what limits and harms them.[1]

It was 2003 and I had just finished *Girlfighting*, a book about how the pressure to conform to narrow feminine ideals combines with long-held stereotypes of women as deceitful and catty to create the conditions for horizontal violence—that is, when girls are angry about being treated unfairly, they take out their anger on one another—"horizontally"—rather than on those responsible for the unfair treatment in the first place. The tidal wave of zero-tolerance policies and top-down disciplinary bully-prevention approaches was just beginning to crash ashore at schools across the country. Along with my students and a colleague, Mary Madden, we began developing a curriculum that would offer middle-school girls opportunities to critically explore and challenge issues they were confronting in school—harassment, stereotypes, bias, and discrimination.

We approached our Girls Coalition Group hoping to create what philosopher Nancy Fraser termed "counterpublic spaces"[2] for girls to talk honestly with one another, name indignities, double standards, and injustices they lived with every day. These were in-school groups and we anticipated resistance from the powers that be. Certainly, school administrators might not see the value in a coalition of girls who question gender injustice and challenge school-sanctioned inequities and exclusions. But we also knew that these same administrators were baffled by a media-hyped "mean girl" crisis they felt increasing pressure to address. We called our approach "bully prevention" and the doors opened.[3]

Four white middle-class women, a professor and her three students, met for an hour each week with seven girls the school identified as "at risk": six white girls and one girl of color living in the poorest neighborhood in our small central-Maine city. We arranged our chairs in a circle, invited the girls to suggest issues they wanted to talk about, and then we tried different ways to open these experiences up, to reflect critically on how and why things happen the way they do, and to imagine what we might do to address them. Our one rule was that we got to be ourselves in the group. We made space to play and have fun and we did not restrict strong feelings, shush loud voices, or monitor language.

Together we developed skit scenarios from the girls' school stories, discussed excerpts from their favorite movies, analyzed music lyrics, and adapted activities we found in books on teaching for social justice. So when conversations about boys began skirting the edges of sexual harassment, we borrowed an activity called "Flirting or Hurting" from gender-justice educator and researcher Nan Stein.[4] We paired it with an activity we modified from a diversity training in which participants, standing side by side, step forward across an imaginary line in response to a series of statements about the forms of harassment they've experienced. The result was a pivotal moment for the girls and for us. Megan, one of the group's facilitators, explains:

> So we were doing the "cross-the-line" activity and we noticed that every single girl in our group had some experience with sexual harassment in their school. And the girls noticed that too and they got really upset about it. They were just learning to consider it sexual harassment as opposed to flirting and they were starting to get pissed because they thought, "Well, this is why this behavior doesn't feel good to us because it's actually harassment; it's not flirting." And they said, "There's got to be some sort of policy about this." They all got their student handbook at the beginning of the year, so we went through it and found that there was a policy for student-teacher harassment but no policy for student-to-student harassment.

This maybe wasn't so unusual in 2003, but we were taken aback. The girls decided they wanted to write a student policy for the handbook and also to raise awareness, so other students in their school could identify for themselves the differences between flirting and hurting.

It hadn't actually occurred to us before this point to do anything more than provide space for girls to talk and think critically about their school experiences. But the girls' passion for making change made total sense, and it was infectious. The ensuing discussion, design, and implementation of the action took several weeks. It was not pretty; this was new territory for all of us. We made things up as we went along, which meant a lot of do-overs and rookie mistakes. We didn't always listen well, we sometimes chose activities that didn't resonate, and we constantly had to remind ourselves to step back and allow the girls to shape conversations. But we hung in there and we did our best to think through the kind of change the girls wanted to see in their school and how they could effect that change. In the end, the girls wrote and delivered to the school board a student-to-student sexual harassment policy that both addressed their experiences and reflected their understanding of the issues in their school.

Today, such policies are mandated. Middle- and elementary-school girls in the more than twenty local Girls Coalition Groups that Hardy Girls now runs don't have to create these policies; instead they are likely to focus their energy on their application and impact. Do they protect nonbinary-gender or gender-nonconforming students, for example? Do they shore up sexual double standards? Are some who report sexual harassment dismissed while others are taken more seriously? There is never a shortage of issues. There are always ways the girls' public schools can do better to ensure fair and equal treatment, become safer and more inclusive spaces.

To engage in activism is, in philosopher and educator Maxine Greene's view, to imagine the world as if it could be otherwise,[5] to engage the immediate—the girls we work with, the issues that matter to them, the contexts they struggle within, the injustices they endure—in imaginative ways and envision something new. The safe and affirming spaces we offer, the questions we pose, the options we create are catalysts to critical consciousness, to what Greene calls "wide-awakeness," and to the possibility that their passionate and forceful reactions to unfairness and hurt will unfold in ways that better their lives going forward.

Activism is good for schools and communities. It is also good for girls—in the learning and doing, in the day-to-day process of relationship building, strategizing, and organizing. Participating in an action offers valuable experience and knowledge to every girl, but it offers the most to girls with the fewest opportunities, those who have been led to believe, in myriad ways by too many people in authority, that they have no real power, and who feel, as a result, tossed about by the world around them.

Consider twelve-year-old Tierra. Like many poor white families in central Maine, hers moved frequently, sometimes into homeless shelters as her mother searched for a stable job and affordable housing. Tierra learned to cover her sadness and guard her secrets with a quick temper and defensive posture. So it wasn't a surprise that she was labeled a troublemaker when she enrolled as a sixth grader in yet another junior high. She was suspended from school for fighting with other girls and sent to the principal's office for talking back to teachers. Tierra was not a girl anyone would identify as a positive force for change.

A few months after her arrival, however, Tierra's school counselor chose her to participate in a Girls Coalition Group specifically designed to connect girls as allies and develop their critical thinking skills through social-action projects in their schools. The group, consisting of two college-age facilitators and eight girls, met for an hour each week during the school day. Together the group discussed sexist stereotypes they saw in media and connected them to the sexism they experienced in their lives, and they considered ways to change their school culture to make it less like a daily struggle.

This school had a specific dress code, one the principal referred to as the three Bs: no butts, no boobs, no bellies. The dress code became a common topic for group discussion because Tierra was often targeted in the hallway for dress code violations, like wearing spaghetti-strap tops. One spring day, as some of the girls in the group moved chairs into a circle in preparation for their weekly meeting, Tierra burst into the room, eyes ablaze. She had not been caught in violation of the dress code this day; instead, she had noticed a pattern. Girls who had yet to develop breasts or who were small-chested could wear spaghetti-strap tops without getting caught. Walking through the halls to class, she saw girls wearing prohibited clothing stroll by teachers, even stop to chat with them, while others wearing the same clothing were reprimanded and told to change. This wasn't just about her. It was bigger than her.

A schoolwide dress code based almost entirely on adult surveillance of girls' body parts was not Tierra's primary concern, although it could have been. Her anger was targeted at the unfair application of school policy. It was the simple fact that some girls could wear clothing to school that others could not. This meant some girls were being punished for growing up—for the size and development of their bodies. Something was wrong here; she'd felt it for some time. But now with the help of her group, Tierra had put her finger on the problem.

She and her group members devised an action. They wrote a polite request to the school principal to ensure the dress code was applied fairly. No spaghetti-strap tops should mean no spaghetti-strap tops—for anyone, regardless of body size. Clipboards in hand, she and the other girls spent the rest of the week gathering signatures in support of their request—walking around the school cafeteria during lunch, intercepting students and teachers between classes, and weaving through noisy after-school bus lines. To Tierra's amazement, lots of students and even some staff and teachers signed the document. When the girls submitted the request to the principal, over a third of the school had joined them in their action.

If Tierra's experience of injustice had occurred a year earlier, she might have taken out her rage on the next teacher to catch her breaking the rule; she might have lashed out at the next girl she saw getting away with wearing a spaghetti-strap top. But she had the opportunity to process what she thought and felt about this situation, to link her personal experience to a larger pattern, and to try out a new way to respond. Most important, she was not alone. She had experienced for the first time in school what it meant to work with supportive adults and other girls in coalition. She knew they had her back; she could bring an unformulated idea to her group and she would be taken seriously. She knew she could rage at unfairness in the safety of the group and the girls and women would not turn away, but help her channel her strong feelings into something others could understand and recognize. She had clarity, a new set of skills, and a trusted group of people behind her.

Why Girls Need Activism

The result of any action is hard to predict, of course, but even when it fails, activism raises awareness and gives those involved a richer understanding of what it takes to move people to imagine new possibilities. As author-activist Courtney Martin points out, in an increasingly complex world it's less often about succeeding perfectly than "failing beautifully."[6] Did the dress code policy change immediately? No. But Tierra and the rest of the group planted a seed of discomfort that played a central role in rewriting the school policy just a few years later. Tierra and her group didn't personally benefit, but their failure to make an immediate change was beautiful in other ways. They had the opportunity to work with and trust other girls and adults, to know what it felt like to be taken seriously, and to educate and influence others.

Activism has the power to make schools and communities safer and more welcoming, but here I'd like to consider the impact on girls who engage in the process. Tierra's story, and the stories of other girl activists like her, points to at least six good reasons why we should be engaging girls in activism and social-change work.

1. Participating in activism makes room for girls like Tierra. Activism is, well, active. By its very nature, it requires questioning and critique, risk taking and agency. Defined by qualities like assertiveness, outspokenness, and at times that most unfeminine emotion, anger, girl activists interrupt the sanctioned and rewarded version of feminine girlhood typically associated with niceness, compliance, and accommodation. Conventional femininity and activism "are subversive of one another."[7] This is why so many of the girl activists sociologist Jessica Taft interviewed for her book *Rebel Girls* tie their narratives of becoming activists to stories of leaving girlhood. As Taft explains, "The traits that they most often associate with girls are the opposite of the characteristics they associate with activists." Activists, the girls explain, are people who are "concerned about important issues, care about other people, are confident, independent, and have knowledge about the world around them,"[8] a far cry from a stereotypical girl identified with superficial concerns like consumerism, popularity, and appearance. Facing into this version of femininity, the young women in

Taft's study felt pressed to "articulate 'girl' and 'activist' as mutually conflicting identities."[9]

Girl-generated activism invites this tension between ideal and real, and opens up public space for what anthropologist Signithia Fordham calls "gender diversity."[10] Girl activists embody alternative versions of girlhood. This makes the spaces they occupy safer for *all* girls, but especially for those who, like Tierra, because of enmeshments of race, social class, ability, gender identity, and expression are more likely to be discounted or disciplined for their outspokenness and resistance.

The opposite of gender diversity occurs when girls are pressed to adapt to a narrow set of behaviors by accommodating others' needs and desires, trying to measure up to feminine ideals, or adhering to conventional gender norms. Doing so leads to all kinds of negative health outcomes.[11] Girls exposed to a lot of sexualized imagery of girls and women, for example, are more likely to self-objectify (judge themselves by appearance); show significantly higher rates of depression, anxiety, and dieting behaviors; have lower body-related self-esteem and decreased confidence in math ability.[12] Increased self-objectification correlates with lower grades.[13] Moreover, girls who self-objectify are more likely to justify a sexist system and less likely to work to change that system.[14] In short, idealized femininity is bad for girls. Taft's girl activists were right to escape its limiting confines. But without gender diversity, without an array of positive alternatives to embrace, a rejection of femininity can look like a rejection of girls and what girls know and feel. Such a narrow script presses a girl to give up valuable experiences and opportunities to experiment, debate, and advocate for what she believes in, to abdicate her power to effect change in the world.[15]

Participating in girl-led activism helps to create a climate where gender diversity is visible and valued. Tierra may have had three strikes against her already and no chance at being the perfect or popular girl in her school, but what she learned in her first action gave her the experience of being a girl others took notice of and listened to. In bringing what she knew to the table, becoming a visible and active presence, she also made her school a little safer and healthier for *all* girls.

2. *Through activism, girls learn to give public voice to their desires, strong feelings, and opinions.* Girls who express strong feelings, especially anger, get a bad rap. There's so much pressure for a girl to disown or dampen down less than nice and kind feelings, the expression of which is a clear sign that she takes herself seriously. And yet psychological health for girls is connected to the opportunity to know and express their strong feelings without being ridiculed, shamed, or punished.[16] The costs are not just personal. Psychologists and philosophers alike refer to anger as "the essential political emotion."[17] Thus, "to silence anger may be to repress political speech."[18] Anger, expressed clearly and used constructively, is a resource and motivation for social change; it's at the heart of individual and collective resistance to oppression and inequality. True, Tierra initially used her anger defensively, as a way to survive a series of hostile environments. But anger itself was not the problem for Tierra. In fact, it was a sign that something was terribly wrong. Once she had a safe space to understand and express her feelings, channel those feelings into action, and experience the support of the girls in her group, her justified anger became a source of positive energy.

Activist work brings a coalition of people together who share passion for a common cause. It's work that requires girls to put what they care about, what they know, and what they're good at in service to something bigger than themselves. There is, in this process, an affirmation of passion and an expectation that people will think together and express what they feel as they consider their cause and their plans. There is opportunity for a girl to be the expert on her own experiences, to tell her story, to author her complex life.

Novelist Chimamanda Ngozi Adichie calls us to resist those who tell our stories starting with "secondly," by which she means a secondhand, stereotypical version of who we are, "flattening" our experiences, rendering us one-dimensional and incomplete. Adichie affirms "the power of many stories to create space for a complex life, for something that feels more like our own, like authenticity."[19] It's urgent that we offer girls this power to reject others' version of their lives. In her coalition group, Tierra started with her observations, her experiences, her version of reality. She didn't start with how she'd been defined by others, as the girl who fights and talks back to teachers. And by living her resonant, complex, messy reality out loud in coalition, Tierra found a way to build something with other girls that affirmed her strong feelings and opinions. She found a way to be herself in her school—to live publicly on her own terms—to be fully in the world and thus able to have an impact on the world.

3. **Participating in activism educates girls about how to understand and negotiate "the culture of power."** Educator Lisa Delpit describes the culture of power as the "ways of talking, ways of writing, ways of dressing, and ways of interacting" that "reflect those who have power." Quite simply, she explains, if you don't already know these things, "if you are not already a participant in the culture of power, being told explicitly the rules of that culture makes acquiring power easier."[20] It also makes it less likely that we will blame ourselves or feel personally inadequate when we can see how the rules disenfranchise us or set us up for failure. For many on the margins of middle-class culture, like Tierra, activism provides an education about how things work in school—the ways of being that are valued, supported, and effective there, and how things get done.

At home, Tierra learned that standing her ground, being direct, speaking up, and defending herself were important survival skills. Because her coalition group heard, understood, and valued this knowledge, and because adults in the group were also conversant in the language and modes of the culture of power, Tierra had both a safe place to express her outrage and help translating those feelings into a language and a mode of action that those in power would respond to. Through the development of her action, Tierra learned ways of communicating with adults in the school that her more privileged peers were exposed to growing up in middle-class homes. The skills she needed to organize an effective action—developing a clear and persuasive argument, identifying the people in her school with the power to fairly enforce the dress code policy, thinking through the best ways to connect with her peers and talk with teachers—helped Tierra experience power as a series of relationships and revealed a flowchart of vertical and horizontal connections she didn't before know existed.

Understanding the power structure of her school, she began to make out the tacit norms and once-invisible lines that those in power used to divide public and private, appropriate and inappropriate actions. She did not have to assimilate to or accept this culture to understand and make strategic choices within it—on the contrary, her group was designed to develop critical consciousness. In fact, Tierra's tenacity, anger, fine-tuned sense of injustice, and even the adaptive social skills she had gained from relocating so often, newly channeled through paths considered legitimate in her school, were highly valuable qualities.

Learning how the culture of power works in her school provided Tierra with a lifetime of skills, since the same codes that operate in schools operate in most other privileged (middle-class-sanctioned) institutions. Knowing that useful networks exist, that they operate in certain ways, that power flows in a predictable fashion through most institutions, enables girls to communicate effectively in these systems and get what they need. Years later, pregnant and working at Subway, Tierra was fired because her pregnancy restricted her ability to do certain tasks, like lift heavy boxes. She knew what unfairness felt like and she knew she had options. One day she dropped into the Hardy Girls office to let us know she had a plan. She had connected with a legal aid provider for those on limited incomes. She sued the local Subway franchise for back pay. They settled out of court. We need to know how the system works in order to do well in it, and organizing an action is a great way to know the system.

4. Activism gives to many the kind of education only a relatively few receive. Typically, the opportunity to study an issue deeply and engage in student-led and project-based exploration of a topic is reserved for those in more privileged private schools or in Advanced Placement courses in public schools. Harvard education professor Catherine Snowe argues that real education happens when students are trying to answer a truly engaging question or solve a personally meaningful problem through discussion, reading, writing, and doing.[21] Youth-development researchers refer to this process as "the hidden curriculum of high academic achievement."[22]

Engaging in activism, then, is a vitally important form of "supplementary education" for girls like Tierra, offering them educational opportunities, skills, and forms of "capital" (for example, cultural capital, social capital, human capital) that are readily available to more privileged students.[23] This isn't rocket science. Research and common sense both draw connections between the kind of personal agency activists experience and a sense of efficacy and high achievement.[24] The more students experience efficacy, the more effort they put in;[25] the more power they have to interrogate, influence, or control their environment and lives, the higher their achievement scores.[26]

Fundamentally, this is about belonging, the sense of comfort and ownership all students should experience in school, and it's about power, a feeling of being included in and having an effect on the decisions that affect our lives. Engaging in activism decreases feelings of alienation and increases political self-efficacy by offering connections and possibilities that help counter all the justified reasons girls can feel numb, angry, alienated, and powerless.[27] As Tierra and the other girls in her group began to name and understand the many indignities they experienced, as they "refashioned their distress into drive to transform their educational circumstances,"[28] they began to experience school as *their* space, to feel they belonged, that they had some power to influence this part of the world. This new sense of belonging and empowerment did not go without notice, or scrutiny, on the part of school administrators. Seeing the students together in the halls, laughing together in the cafeteria, working together on their projects, made the school principal nervous, to the extent that he warned the group facilitators about taking a collection of individual tough girls and "making them into a little gang." The principal's concern stemmed from the girls' new visibility as a group—the hallway clusters of activity, the physical space they claimed, their raucous laughter—that is, from their sense of belonging.

Activism invites meaningful exploration of how things work. To consider the root causes of issues and to imagine creating some kind of change requires girls to look beyond immediate experience to see the bigger picture. In doing so, it offers, maybe for the first time, what those raised and educated in more privileged settings experience every day: a sense of being a part of their education, and with this, permission to wonder aloud, to try and fail without judgment, to ask insightful, transgressive questions without being labeled troublesome, to be openly excited about new and promising possibilities, to challenge the way things go.

5. Activism moves girls from passive consumer to active citizen. Media and marketers have sold girls a highly profitable pop culture version of power in which girls are first and foremost consumer citizens and their primary project is to "fix" themselves.[29] Teen- and tween-targeted media co-opt Girl Power discourse, touting the freedom to choose among various shades of lip gloss, the "aspirational" qualities of Victoria's Secret lingerie, and the power to look hot, effectively channeling time, energy, and resources into a "girls just want to have fun" regiment of self-improvement. It's a brilliantly enticing and glitzy cover for a truly anxiety-producing message: being a girl is equivalent to being a failure; you will never measure up. To try requires money and a huge investment of time and energy.

Instead of telling girls that "the key to happiness and success is self-esteem," *Full Frontal Feminism* author Jessica Valenti argues, "we should tell girls the truth": the media-constructed definition of "'beautiful' is bullshit, a standard created to make women into good consumers, too busy wallowing in self-loathing to notice that we're second-class citizens. Girls don't need more self-esteem or feel-good mantras about loving themselves—what they need is a serious does of righteous anger."[30] Inherent in activism is the challenge to look beneath the surface of things, to no longer accept at face value the images, messages, and situations in which a girl finds herself.

Tierra and her group members spent weeks questioning the media messages bombarding them, telling them their worth was in how well they matched up to an ideal that was out of reach, how certain nonconforming bodies invite surveillance and judgment, and how unearned advantages are proffered to those who look and act a narrow version of right. This exploration and critique provided a way to examine all kinds of surface messages, invited the girls to look deeper, to think about what real power feels like and how it works, to consider who makes decisions, who sets priorities and why. Reclaiming Girl Power in this way, separating it out from a consumer version of citizenship that invites her to remake herself, to shop and prettify her world, provides Tierra with something real and solid on which to hang her self-worth.

6. Activism offers girls the power of connection and relationship with other girls and women. In popular culture girls rarely see girls and women working together for social change; instead they watch a steady stream of media girlfighting and drama, usually laced with sexualized imagery and dismissive humor. In fact, what makes groups, like the one Tierra joined, so difficult to facilitate is the barrage of stereotypes about "mean girls" that both girls and adults accept as simple fact. It's also what makes the activist work girls do together so powerful. Nothing interrupts the prevailing discourse of untrustworthy, backstabbing girls better than working through the complicated process of creating an activist project: identifying the root cause of a problem girls share across difference, brainstorming solutions, relying on one

another, getting to know one another's strengths and weaknesses, setting and reaching goals.

Trust issues ran deep in Tierra's group. Every girl in the room had a story of betrayal, abandonment, and hurt. The familiar rhetoric of girlfighting and the realities of adult indifference provided convenient channels for their fear and anger, threatening to pull them apart when they needed one another the most. Accepting without challenge the pervasive and divisive discourse of mean, tough girls would effectively invite Tierra and the girls in her group to engage in horizontal forms of aggression, taking their anger and frustration at their treatment in school out on one another. Their rational response to a hostile environment would most certainly become proof to the school administration that the girls' assertiveness and outspokenness are signs of danger and trouble.

Instead, Tierra and her group discovered a newfound ability to channel their frustration and critique toward injustice rather than toward one another, which provided support in the face of classist and sexist assumptions that circulated through the school. But the girls' increasingly coherent protest of unfair policies challenged the status quo and thus invited adult surveillance. Their principal's expressed concern that the girls were becoming "a little gang" gave permission to teachers to watch for signs of collective trouble and separate the girls when they were too loud or visible. Sharing their strengths and vulnerabilities and identifying the source of their feelings of displacement and alienation offered Tierra and her group the possibility of remaining together instead of splitting apart.

Unlike her middle-class peers, who are likely to experience school as a kind of home away from home, a place where teachers reflect parental values and the environment supports what they already know about how to maneuver in the world,[31] Tierra felt disconnected and alienated when she transferred to her new school. Finding others she could talk with, think with, laugh and take up space with, while a visible disruption to the middle-class flow of the school, gave Tierra a sense that this was a place she could be, that she could want to be, and these were girls she could be herself with. Tierra experienced the kind of connectedness researchers tell us is so vital to healthy development and that derives from the opportunity to be seen and respected, from the power to influence others, and the sense that she mattered in her school.[32]

Intergenerational Interventions

Adrienne Rich once wrote, "Connections between and among women are the most feared, the most problematic and the most potentially transformative force on the planet."[33] This is true for women only if, as girls, they witness the power of such connections and experience loyalty in the moments when our work together is challenged, when the powers that be insist on naming the girls we work with or the work we do together as the problem.

Activist work in public settings like schools and communities is an interruption, it shifts meaning, it disrupts assumptions. Such work requires women to step up, to listen, to work with girls and intervene on their behalf—to act strategically and use our privilege, our power, and our connections when necessary. When Tierra's group drew negative attention from the principal and was in jeopardy of being disbanded, the group facilitators initiated a series of conversations with school administrators and it was allowed to continue. Transformative connections between women begin with experiences of loyalty and bravery between women and girls. Standing with them, standing up for them, transformed the way things usually went between women and the girls in Tierra's group. For many of the girls, this shift toward trusting relationships with one another and with their adult muses trumped anything else the group accomplished.

In her interviews with youth activists from across the Americas, Jessica Taft heard girls talk about "disheartened and inactive" adults in their homes, schools, and communities who had given up, who had "ceased to believe in the possibility of change."[34] In the face of adults who "have stopped dreaming big," girls choose to go it alone, believing "if they want the world to be different, they are going to have to start trying to change it themselves, today."[35] This is testament to girls' passion, courage, and tenacity, but going it alone is not a viable option. Our best chance of addressing injustice and making lasting improvements is to work together, across generations.

We are led to believe that intergenerational feminist work isn't possible. With each wave that crashes ashore, we lose sight of the ocean. Media, in love with a good catfight or mother-daughter betrayal or adult versus youth story, focus on our disagreements as if they are irreconcilable differences. As if we are not stronger when we openly debate, when we challenge one another. As if the criticality so fundamental to social change ever happens outside passionate and committed relationships. In part 2 of this book, girls and women activists offer guideposts, provide pathways, and share what it looks and feels like to work together. They believe in the possibility of change. They dream big. They know the ability to make dreams come true depends on intergenerational alliances, mutual respect, and a set of conditions forged over time and in relationship.

PART TWO

NECESSARY CONDITIONS

Intergenerational collaborations are difficult. If we ourselves have not experienced such partnerships, it's not something we are likely to know how to do very well. There are few models. If we currently work with youth, we're more likely to find ourselves in traditional settings, schools and other organizations, where adults are fully in charge and it's an interruption to invite girls' critical voices and opinions to the table; where youth (and adults) who openly challenge norms, question decisions, or resist policies are considered uncooperative, a disruption, a problem to address. In the absence of ready-made spaces for this kind of work, we have to seek out and join with others who share what we value and who see the developmental and the political importance of engaging in intergenerational forms of activism.

When we insist on listening to and taking seriously what girls have to offer, a set of tensions inevitably surface around power and control. We come up against common forms of adultism, a belief system that includes, in the words of sociologist Jessica Taft, "all of the behaviors and attitudes that flow from the assumption that adults are better than young people and are entitled to act upon young people in many ways without their agreement."[1] It's a challenge to this belief system to insist on girls' right to voice their thoughts and feelings about practices and policies that affect them, and it's a challenge, often to our colleagues and friends, when we offer guidance, experiences, education, tools, and resources that expand girls' self-determination.[2] We are in conflict with cultural assumptions about what girls are capable of and what they have a right to ask for, and we confront stereotypes about girls who question and resist the ways things go. In our support for such girls, we are likely to experience a good bit of mansplaining about the importance of current structures and systems to the well-being of children.[3]

So how do we begin? One step is to learn from experienced others who have been engaged in the work over time and who can offer guidance. The series of chapters that follow arose out of in-depth conversations with nineteen girls and young women and eight adult women, all experienced activists involved in a "transformative model" of civic engagement—that is, they do their work across generations with the intent to "change the conditions of their schools, communities, and the broader social contexts in which they live."[4] I chose these activists because I know a good bit about their work and the organizations they work within, and I believe they represent the kind of progressive feminist approaches that both dignify girls and move us toward social justice. They are diverse with respect to age, race, sexual orientation, and geography; they do their activism online and on the ground, in urban, suburban, and rural contexts. They differ in ways I try to honor, but they share a commitment to intergenerational partnerships as a way to make the world a better place.[5] As stated in this book's introduction, the following chapters are not designed to be a "how-to" but a "how-to-be"—how to be in relationship, how to be open to possibility, how to be aware of our own biases and assumptions, how to be someone who works collaboratively and effectively with girls. There is no blueprint. There is no one-size-fits-all approach to this kind of intergenerational work. But the themes that reverberate in the interviews with these women and girls began to feel like a set of necessary conditions for doing this work well—for being in this work honestly and humbly and with integrity. Each of the following chapters explores a theme, a necessary condition; some pertain more to girls, others to women, but all those interviewed agree on their importance.

This is about doing; it's about the practice of being in relationship and creating environments that enable girls to know and experience their power. Each time we do this work, it is different; each time, it feels like we're making it up.[6] Because we are moving beyond things as they exist to imagining things as they could be,[7] this work is inherently creative and messy and unpredictable. Each time, the girls we work with are different, the conditions are different, *we* are different. And yet, with practice, we learn to anticipate problems and possibilities. We are quicker to predict the emergence of old habits and justifications, better able to address familiar forms of institutional sediment. Time and again we clear away debris caused by the same old protective good intentions, but even so, we cannot come in fully prepared for the unknown and the unexpected.

Seeing how activists—girls and adults—engage "the relational messiness,"[8] how they react and respond to the unexpected, offers something more like a way of seeing, listening, and reacting than it does a set of operating instructions. For all the differences in the focus and content of their work, the variations in their histories and training, a pattern of tensions and negotiations seems to emerge from complex, seemingly incongruous experiences. For the women, especially, these patterns present a series of balancing acts: identifying with girls without living through them; offering support without taking over; enabling girls' agency and guiding them in hostile situations; being fully present and relinquishing control.

I say this upfront because I suspect readers will want more advice, more direction, more specifics than what is offered in these next chapters. This is a field guide, after all. But girls and women offer no relational equivalent to identifying a plant or bird—nothing like specific colors, songs, and territories we can identify and record. Instead I offer examples of contradictions and balancing acts and relational options. I offer a way of being, a way of approaching and analyzing situations that pop up, and that's not going to feel specific enough. If it's any comfort, it never feels specific enough—to me or to any of the girls and women in this book. You are in good company. But I can offer one truth. All the forces motivating our desire to work together to address injustice—passion, anger, respect, a desire for a more loving world—demand "the kind of analysis that says that what you believe in is worthwhile for human beings in general, and in the future."[9] Our work with girls is, first and foremost, about this faith and this analysis.

CHAPTER FOUR

Beyond Gloria Steinem

A Rich Feminist History

"The quickest way to silence a mouth is to treat it as if none have come before," say Dominique Christina and Denice Frohman, the spoken word duo known as Sister Outsider Poetry, in their powerful piece "No Child Left Behind."[1] This is because history, what comes before, connects us to ourselves, positions us in time and place, broadens and deepens and contextualizes the issues we share and struggle with in this present moment. Girls with a history of activism to draw from have a clarity, an understanding, a more intricate language to explain what they experience. The issues in their lives become part of a larger whole and they are not left floating about, unmoored, wondering if what matters to them has ever mattered to anyone else. Wondering if any girl like them has ever made a difference.

Learning about activists who came before, especially girl activists, is an energizing and motivating force. Girls in the civil rights movement, the women's movement, the labor movement, offer connections and a sense of responsibility and urgency to continue the work. "I know that is why we are here, based on what happened before," says fifteen-year-old Julia, thinking back to the women's movement she's learning about as part of SPARK. "I don't want it to stop. There's still so much that needs to happen."

> I wish I had learned about it a little more, because in school you talk about, like, women's suffrage, but you don't really talk about anything in between. I heard about famous feminists who came before me and I know, you know, that was really important and we are continuing that in different ways through the Internet and taking different approaches to it. But I wish there could be more, like, history lessons I guess, about feminists who came before us and what they did. I definitely think knowing what they did continues their goals and their dreams into the future and onto the next generation and through different mediums like social media and stuff like that. So we are bringing it to a different level I guess, and that definitely inspires me to keep doing all the activism that we do with SPARK and Hardy Girls. I want to continue that movement.

Girls are more likely to learn these history lessons from episodes of Comedy Central's *Drunk History* than they are in school. On that silly "liquored-up narration of our nation's history"[2] they'll learn more about Mary Dyer, Mary Ellen Pleasant, Sybil Ludington, Edith Wilson, and Claudette Colvin than they ever will in their sober classrooms. Neither will they learn about the history of issues that affect their daily lives, from racial profiling to sexual harassment to reproductive rights to pay inequities. It's a rare teacher who connects #BlackLivesMatter to the Student Nonviolent Coordinating Committee's role in the civil rights movement, and rarer still for a teacher to connect #SayHerName to the experiences of young women in the SNCC. The girls say they feel disenfranchised because they have so little history and so few models to learn from, so few opportunities to contextualize and connect with what's right in front of them.

As philosopher Peggy McIntosh, historian Howard Zinn,[3] and others remind us, the history taught in school is told from the perspective of those in power, and for the most part this version has "left out the female half of humankind, and excluded the knowledge of most people of color worldwide about their own cultures and their versions of history."[4] It also deemphasizes how women, working people, and people of color have worked together within organized social movements to shape history. If social change "is made not by a few heroic individuals, but instead by people's choices and actions," as the Zinn Education Project website proclaims, then our "own choices and actions matter."[5]

In the absence of full public stories about what girls and young women have accomplished in the face of violence, oppression, and discrimination, the activism they engage in—pushing back on school dress codes, culture-jamming sexist and racist media, advocating for gender-neutral bathrooms—is misunderstood, maligned, and joked about, even by their friends. In school they experience others' disdain for the feminist lens that has been so eye-opening and important to them. As a result, Julia says, she and the other SPARKteam girls spend a lot of time "dispelling myths of feminism." "They don't understand it," agrees Samantha, an eighteen-year-old Latina known to her friends as Sam. "'Are you a lesbian?' 'Do you wear bras?' It's something they don't want to be labeled as." It's so important, says Yas Necati, sixteen years old and white, to "provide opportunities for girls to go out and learn about feminism. Because right now we are on our own."

> I guess we are sort of sent messages from a young age about how we should be, and feminism sort of counters most of that. So I guess it's hard because the majority of people feel a certain way and actually criticize feminism because it's sort of not what everyone thinks. Feminism in general is seen as a dirty word and seen as bad; it has a lot of negative connotations because of the way the media has portrayed it. And I think a lot of people absorb this and we just don't take the time or the space to properly educate people about feminism.

A large part of the problem is the absence of any but the most superficial education about feminism in history books. Yas, who edits the feminist online magazine *Powered by Girl,*[6] and who advocates for comprehensive sexuality education in the UK, is frustrated with the little she's been taught about feminism in school.

> We will get, like, one history lesson where a quarter of the hour is taken up about the suffrage acts. "This is what happened." And they will speak about it as something that was in the past, something that did happen and was good back then but doesn't really exist anymore. Like there is nothing in schools about it. Really the only way young people will learn about feminism is if they go out and look for it themselves.

As a result, many of the girls do their own research, connect with others online, seek out the histories that provide significance to their experiences and concerns so they can, as sociologist Jessica Taft says, "feel connected to larger social struggles, giving them a sense of the importance of their contemporary work."[7] Such awareness emboldens them to speak their truths with full knowledge of who they stand with, where they fit in, and what they contribute, so they know whether they are adding a pebble to a growing pile or beginning a landslide of new ideas. "Knowing that others have come before them, and when others haven't come before," is important to Ileana Jiménez, a high school English teacher who has developed a well-respected course on feminism and activism at her progressive independent high school, because "they don't always necessarily see that they are the pioneers." Jiménez's passion is in helping her students know their power as social-change agents by creating a wide range of opportunities for them to learn from experienced activists and to make connections between theory and practice.[8]

In the absence of lessons learned in school, Joanne Smith, a Haitian American social worker who founded and directs the intergenerational grassroots organization Girls for Gender Equity (GGE), a New York City–based nonprofit, takes her responsibility to educate the girls of color she works with about feminism, anti-racist advocacy, and youth activism very seriously.

> Our job is to teach them by keeping the history of our movements alive and by directing them to resources. We're here and we're educators and while they teach us a lot, we have a responsibility to them, to have conversations about the history of feminism and women's rights, about racism and all of the oppression we're faced with, because many times they come to us with that hunger and that desire to learn more about what they're not learning in school.

Our role in the work, Smith says, is to "lend our history . . . and help [girls] get a sense of what they are becoming a part of," both in the widest sense and also within the local GGE programs she directs. "It's important to have that understanding that there's a legacy of young people who have done really great work here, and you're a part of that legacy by being in Sisters in Strength," she maintains. "These young people have done the work with integrity, and we know that they will carry it on." Amber, sixteen and a member of Sisters in Strength, GGE's two-year program for youth organizers, appreciates what it means to be part of this history, to engage with work that's "based on what was happening before we came, and something that will go on throughout the years."

Girls need this history if they are to be effective activists, and feminism, if it is to become a vibrant, intersectional movement, needs them to know it and use it. "They need real knowledge about the issues they're activating around," explains Dana Edell, who is white and SPARK's executive director, and this includes where they fit within the history of feminism:

> So many weak movements fold and dissolve because they try to bring young people in and they don't even really know what they're fighting for. . . . We need to help them learn about these issues. They need to learn some of the history of the movement.

> One thing that we keep telling them [at SPARK] and that we try to
> tell them in our training is, "You're not the first girls in history to
> recognize sexism and try to do something about it, and so, let's try
> to learn from successful and challenging movements in the past."

Feminist organizer Shelby Knox, known for her work advocating for comprehensive sex education in her Lubbock, Texas, high
school,[9] conducted one of the first feminist-history workshops
SPARK offered the team of girls. Knox, passionate about girls' and
women's history, had just developed the Radical Women's History
Project,[10] because, she says,

> I've always loved history and as I got older and more feminist,
> I found myself asking more and more often, "Where are the
> women?" I felt like I was missing a part of myself by not know-
> ing how the women before me lived and worked and fought for
> social change. As I started to do more research to fill this hole,
> I realized that the women's history we *do* honor is often that of
> white, Western, straight, cisgender, able-bodied women, which
> is the same story of privileging only privileged experiences that
> has propped up patriarchy for centuries. The goal [of the Radical
> Women's History Project] is simple: rewrite ALL women back
> into history so we can collectively and individually know what is
> possible for ourselves.[11]

Knox's workshop widened the girls' field of vision, opening them
up to all the ways their histories are missing, inviting richer conversations about difference and deeper conversations about the
importance and power of visibility and resistance.

Not surprisingly, the girls came out of the workshop enlight-
ened and energized. Building on Women's History Month, they
developed an action they called Women's History Year. Melissa
Campbell, programming coordinator for SPARK and a former
member of the SPARKteam herself, explains: "We asked girls to
ask people in their lives—to interview their friends and family, or

if they're feeling particularly bold, interview a stranger—about the women who really inspire them, both historical women and women who they know personally. And the results have been really amazing. I read about a lot of women I had no idea about. That is super cool."[12]

From that point on, feminist activist history became a part of the SPARKteam's training, inspiring a range of actions designed to uncover the powerful work of women too often overlooked. Led by one of the SPARKteam members, eighteen-year-old Joneka, the girls developed Black Women Create, highlighting women in the film and television industries "who are telling their own stories and who are creating complex and diverse Black female characters that are relatable and accurate."[13]

When the girls heard about Field Trip, Google's location-based app designed to alert travelers when they are near historical landmarks, they created Women on the Map, which points out the often-forgotten sites of women's contributions to history.[14] Together the girls and adult staff mapped and wrote profiles of over a hundred women, connecting their stories to locations in dozens of cities and twenty-eight countries around the world.

The SPARK training and the ensuing actions were personally transformative for the girls. Seeing the connections between her experiences of activism and a rich feminist past "was just such an awakening," team member Izzy says, and offered "a huge education network" she had no idea existed. Izzy, who is Jewish, was just fourteen and in eighth grade when she joined SPARK and "didn't know much about women's issues at all."

> I remember going to my first SPARK retreat and just sitting down in the workshops and hearing all the speakers talking about, you know, women's issues and history and stuff and being like "Oh my God!" It was such an awakening because, like, I didn't *know*. I mean, I knew who Gloria Steinem was, and I knew who some of the people that they were talking about were and some of the issues but I wasn't even seeing it in that kind of light.

After years of formal schooling, years of worksheets, lectures, and standardized tests, learning relationally and interactively with other girls and women about something so real and personal was enlightening. When Edell organized a feminist workshop styled after the TV quiz show *Jeopardy*, Izzy was all in.

Her initial ignorance of women's history felt like an invitation to Izzy, not a judgment. Izzy talks about being "inspired" by and connected to feminists and girl activists who came before, like Samantha Smith, whose 1982 letter to Soviet premier Yuri Andropov had such a profound impact on the Cold War.

> She was, I think, eleven when she wrote the letter. It was almost like we were kind of following in her footsteps with girl-led activism in Maine. And Malala Yousafzai, I just look at her and think, "Wow. You are an inspiration." I think about Shelby Knox and how when she got involved she was fifteen and that's how old I am. And she got so much more hate then I did. She was trying to promote, you know, sex education in the most conservative town in Texas. She was publicly ridiculed by national talk show hosts and stuff. And when I think about that and that she's still doing activism work and she's still so young and she hasn't been brought down. Just like all of these feminists in history who have had so much backlash and they're still going. I think that is so inspirational.

As Izzy learns about girl activists, both past and present, as she identifies with some and is inspired by others, she begins to put in perspective the consequences of speaking up and making waves. In the end, Izzy says, "I think one of the most important lessons these women have taught me is just like it's more important to do this work than it is to feel bad."

> You know, you can be hurt by this, but your feelings don't really matter in the long run, because one person can say something mean to you and that sucks and then you could give up, but who are *you* in this? You are one of the awesome women

working towards this cause and if you're going to give up and let the whole domino effect of everyone else fall down because you decide that, you know, it kind of sucks and you don't like it anymore. . . . You should, you know, try not to take things so personally and realize that you're part of a team and you're going to get hate. But it's more worth it for the end result than just to back out and feel good about yourself temporarily.

When adult activists working with girls take the time to connect the dots, fill in the missing pieces, reclaim history as our history, we arm girls with stories of resistance, bravery, and daring, reveal the important connections between causes and tactics, shore them up with a past that helps them see and name and respond to what's in front of them. In turn, girls take their newfound knowledge to their schools and communities in ways that are surprising, even to them. For SPARKteam member Celeste Montaño, nineteen, there's nothing quite like an activist project to deepen awareness and understanding, even for those who thought they had a handle on a problem. Celeste, Latina, took the lead on a campaign to diversify Google Doodles, discussed in chapter 9. The campaign had a profound impact, bringing "to my attention what I hadn't been thinking about too much. Like whose history we learn and how we learn history. I think that's going be kind of like a passion I will follow throughout my life." She not only discovered amazing women she'd never learned about in school, but the work of researching the history of those included in Doodles opened her up to another level of analysis:

> When we tried to sort people or label people by race, [I learned] how incredibly complicated that was. It was definitely a learning experience. Like I would totally have agreed with you if you told me that race was a social construct, even before the Google Doodles action. But just actually seeing how completely impossible it is to really truly label someone one thing or another, that was like really hugely eye-opening.

This work is, at its best, intergenerational—we chip away at the pieces in front of us while remaining aware of the larger framework and where we fit in. "When I first joined Sisters in Strength, I didn't think it would be this all-encompassing," Amber explains. She and fellow African American activist Cheyanne, both sixteen, talk about how what they learned in Sisters in Strength revealed the way power and oppression work and helped them name and respond to racism in their school. They began to ask questions, to talk about their experiences with other girls in the program. "Sharing stories helps us understand," Cheyanne says. Sharing stories reveals patterns. And patterns reveal in our schools and communities systems created over time. "I think we know [racism] is a real problem because a majority of us do not go to the same school," Amber explains. "And the fact that every single person comes back like, 'Yeah, that happens in my school.' We got all sorts of different people here, and we know it's a problem."

Teaching history is important, but so is providing the collective support and training for girls to research and examine together the evolution of the issues they care about. On the SPARKteam's blog there is information about the Black Women Create series, movies and books about brave girls and women, many of whose stories are little-known, profiles of grandmothers who marched with Betty Friedan, and inspiring histories of movements like the Guerrilla Girls and Riot Grrrls, which continue to influence girl-led feminism.[15] These materials immerse girls in the complexity of the issues in front of them as they have developed over time. As GGE's Joanne Smith says:

> If social justice issues were solvable by an organization that did work for ten, fifteen, or twenty years, then we wouldn't have social justice issues because the great fifty- and one-hundred-plus-years organizations that came before ours would have solved them by now. There were those embodying social justice frameworks before they were born. Before we were even conscious of

oppressive and liberating frameworks. It's important for youth to understand that this is lifelong work and to see that they are contributing to paving a path for generations following them.

Girls who bring all their power and integrity to this moment, shored up by others who once shared their passion to make the world a more just place, find great pleasure in bringing along the next generation. "Since I've become an activist," Yas says, "I do have young girls come up to me and ask me about stuff." In response, she offers a history lesson, or rather, a lesson she has learned about history from doing activist work. "We are all in this together," she says. "If any of the great people who have made massive differences in history were like, 'What can I do? I am just one person,' then we wouldn't have had so many amazing things happen. We all want the same things and we are all fighting against the same backlash. So it's a collective struggle and whatever age, it is the same."

CHAPTER FIVE

Good Intentions Aren't Enough

Genuine Relationships

A few years ago, while observing a Buddhist monk create and then destroy a sand mandala at my college's art museum, I was struck by the similarities that exist between his process and women's work with girl activists. Certainly not with respect to the energy, noisiness, and occasional near-chaos of partnering with girls, and not just with the patience it takes to build a richly layered project, although there's surely that. It was more the life lessons in impermanence and loss. After weeks of passionate commitment to something beautiful, the monk poured the sand into water to disperse the mandala's energy. Working with girl activists feels a little like this. So much time and energy intensely focused on this creative thing in front of us and then a series of letting goes—of attachment, control, investment—as girls take over and the work ripples out into the world, traveling who knows where, inciting who knows what, inspiring as-yet-unimaginable responses and reactions.

Intergenerational activism is both wildly imaginative and solidly grounded; it's about the give and take of relationships, the constant need for thoughtful negotiation, the beautiful failures and surprising opportunities. Doing such work well, by which I don't mean perfectly, is about learning how to be present and open in the face of uncertainty. It's not a science. It's a practice. Skills are cultivated by being in relationship, showing up and participating, failing, adjusting, and showing up again. And since no two relationships are alike, the skills cultivated are more about how to be fully present and helpful in each new situation. Perhaps the best way to describe this is a Zen-like coming to our senses. Girl activists say they want the adults they work with to be real, by which they mean, in SPARK-team member Izzy's words, "not fake." They want women who know them and who they can trust with that knowledge; women they feel "relationally close" to and with whom they have "deep personal connections." Such women "listen," says Alice, seventeen and a member of SPARK for several years, and they "talk to teenagers like they're people and not projects." They "don't make assumptions about our lives and about our ideas. They give girls the benefit of the doubt." There's a generosity of spirit in this way of being in relationship. Such an adult is like a "close pal," Izzy says, and like close pals, her fellow SPARKteam member Julia, fifteen, adds, they "share their experiences," not as a way to suggest what's right, but to let girls know "different perspectives are welcomed."

Girls define such trusted adults by comparing them with those they don't feel genuine connections with, those who discipline them for speaking up or who act like they know what matters, but couldn't possibly because they have not been paying close attention. "With other adults you can't just blurt out strong opinions," says Cassidy, who is white, seventeen, and a member of the Girls Advisory Board (GAB) for Hardy Girls Healthy Women. Other adults "get scared when girls get angry and riled up or heated and excited; they think there are consequences to that" asserts twenty-two-year-old Ty, who is white and, as one of the oldest SPARK-team members, assumed a mentoring role with younger members. Measured against these experiences, it's both unusual and welcome when the women activists they work with "allow passion," says another SPARKteam member, Montgomery, who is eighteen and biracial (black/white). Women who remain open and present when girls express strong feelings, girls say, allow them to "feel safe" and "comfortable." Such women reserve judgment. They "learn from girls—that we feel things 'really deeply' but not in a teenager dramatic kind of way," Alice explains. These kinds of relationships are so rare that they can feel kind of illicit. Adults who are "real" talk about "stuff no one's going to tell you in school," Alice says. "Like people don't really talk to you about the prison industrial complex in high school, and it feels so much more like, you're kind of getting away with something. And it's just so powerful. It changes your whole world."

Building genuine relationships with girls requires adults to show up as complete human beings, willing to talk about tough issues, share interests, experiences, flaws—letting girls in on who we are. Teacher Ileana Jiménez talks about how important it is to share "all those parts of me . . . the Latina, queer, woman part of me" with her high school student activists. Coming to activist work whole invites her students to do the same and to think how being fully present "affects them"—informs the issues they feel passionate about and the ways they choose to engage those issues. Being real with girls requires "you to be real with yourself," explains Amina Harris (not her real name), Girls for Gender Equity's community organizer. This means resisting the impulse "to compartmentalize" or "not be your full self" in girls' presence. Being fully present, fully human, makes it possible for girls to be their complicated, imperfect selves and to see the power of being on their own side. As someone who graduated from Sisters in Strength, the program she now facilitates, Harris says, "it's really important for me to be very open with my identity as a black woman, as a queer woman, as a young person, as a slowly but surely no-longer-being-a-young-person."

> It's important for me to share those pieces of myself with the young women that I work with because they really value those parts of me, and they learn to value all the parts of themselves, like being able to talk about body image and being able to talk

about the things that we don't feel great about all of the time. It's really important because so often they get all this imagery, you know, of either you are a terrible, terrible person or you are like Beyoncé, perfect, superhuman, that dichotomy. And it's just like, "No, you don't have to be Michelle Obama. You can be you. Whoever you want to be is important and vital to the work, because without you the work wouldn't work the way it does."

Sharing who we are, owning our strengths and our vulnerabilities and inviting theirs, creates pathways out of the "perfect success or terrible failure" dichotomy that can so trap girls. But even for those who have worked with girl activists for years, this is difficult. Truth be told, Dana Edell explains, "I think the adults are often not as honest with girls as we ask the girls to be with us, especially when we're failing."

I think adults get a little scared, they either want to be the cool adult all the time and so they don't want to say what they're really thinking at the moment, or we don't want the girls to think we don't understand. I think it's equally important that the girls see that, like, "Oh shit, the grownups made a mistake," that we weren't able to follow through with something that we said; we messed up. I think that's incredibly powerful for girls to see that we take this responsibility when we fail.

Girls are watching. Observing such honest moments, Izzy says she learns, "Hey, it is all right to screw up." Melissa Campbell, SPARK's program coordinator, agrees. "I think it is so important, the ability to fuck up and not have your entire world come crashing down."

Risking our whole selves is humbling; admitting our fears and struggles is anxiety-producing. But there is no other way to be in genuine relationships. "I think many times it looks scary," Joanne Smith says about her work with girls at Girls for Gender Equity. "It looks like you don't know, you know, and you don't want them to fail, but they will fail, and it will hurt, and you will still be there, and you will be honest about your failure."

Being honest about failure is a complicated thing. It means we admit our imperfections, yes. But it also demands that we talk honestly about how we are positioned within systems of power and privilege and how this affects who we are and how we struggle. When Ileana Jiménez shares "all those parts of me," she offers her students the experiences of a teacher who, like many of them, grew up in a working-class family and who was, like many of them will be, a first-generation college student. She embodies the power of education. Her ethnicity, gender, class, and sexuality are always at play in her classroom. As a queer feminist teacher of color, she invites a complex conversation about intersectionality, about systems of oppression and privilege that set some up to fail and others to succeed. Being in authentic relationships means struggling openly with these aspects of identity and dimensions of difference that make us who we are. We have to go there, Smith says, "because they are always watching you. It's a humbling position to be working with young people in an honest way, but it can be the most rewarding work you do if you allow yourself to do it."

Girls pick up on the tension and uncertainty we experience but don't speak. They read the fear and the judgments we carry into our relationships. We are especially accountable in these moments when girls feel, as Julia says, "kind of hesitant to speak about our problems," or when it's difficult for them to "directly disagree with someone else, like especially if it's an adult." It is our responsibility to appreciate and address the borders between us, especially when we are working with girls across difference. This is an issue nineteen-year-old Celeste, who is Latina, thought a lot about when she joined SPARK Movement three years earlier. Because it was hard for her to raise issues of race with the white adults in the organization, she imagined how tough it would be for someone much younger.

Sometimes adults don't realize the weight that their words hold with younger girls, but especially younger girls of color, since white authority figures can be super intimidating. I mean, a fourteen-year-old is going to have a different perspective on adult fallibility than a twenty-one-year-old. It's hard for anyone to call out a figure of authority, particularly regarding stuff like race, but younger girls especially are used to just ignoring their own discomfort and listening to what adults say. Because their relationship with adults in school and at home is largely about respect and not challenging authority, they're much less likely to speak up if something feels wrong. Often girls tend to think they're the ones in the wrong.

Knowing Ourselves

Opening ourselves to genuine relationship with girls is about seeing who they are and not who we think they should be. Addressing this barrier between what is and what we think or want is our work, not theirs. When asked to give advice to adults who want to support girl activists, fifteen-year-old Lily, who is white and a member of GAB, says, "Know yourself!" For Smith, "this means starting with yourself as an adult, and challenging your own ageism and your own internalized sexism or internalized racism, or racism if you are not a person of color, and being able to like, look at that honestly and speak about that honestly." This is the hard personal work required before we can hope to negotiate the borders that risk genuine connections with girls.[1] Jiménez agrees. Good intentions aren't enough. "You have to do a lot of homework," she says. "You can't just be passionate about 'giving girls a voice.' I think that can be cliché and kind of almost patronizing. You need to understand the responsibility that comes with providing young people a platform to find that voice."

As eighteen-year-old Treva, who is white and has been a member of GAB since she was thirteen, says, adults who have met that responsibility, who have reflected on issues of power and privilege, who move into relationships with girls prepared to learn and make mistakes, are more likely to "come with a sense of when to engage and when to let it happen." They are aware that "giving girls a voice" means acknowledging where we end and they begin; respecting the in-between where surprising things happen, but only if we are ready and willing to remain open.

Girls say they can tell when adults aren't in this open place. "I'll talk to them about the issues, and sometimes I can just tell that their heart, maybe, isn't in the right place," SPARKteam member Katy, who is eighteen and Asian American, says. "And that's really what activism is about; the heart needs to be in the right place." Girl activists are looking for both emotional and intellectual honesty, and they often judge this by how possible it is to talk about the hard things with women, to "speak up about issues," Julia says, and "express strong opinions," Cassidy adds. The litany that girls offer about the women they love sounds familiar across interviews. They are people who are "upfront and real," someone "you can disagree with and there are no hard feelings," someone "not afraid to give me critique or be like, 'I know you can.' They push me. I want to get better and [they] help with that." This all requires the safety and knowledge that comes with real relationships. "Only someone who really knows me," Celeste says, knows how to "push beyond my comfort zone, but not so much that I want to give up."

If we invite girls to name and address the daily indignities and injustices they experience, we will find ourselves in the presence of strong feelings. We need to know ourselves on this front too. "Opening up genuine connections can be scary and difficult to manage without shutting down," SPARK executive director Dana Edell says. "I think, rage . . . I think girls realize, once they see the injustice around them, they see how unfair certain things in the world are. Adolescents have an acute barometer of unfairness— 'That's fucking not fair!'" It can be hard not to be defensive in those moments, especially because we as adults are often implicated in their anger. We are often invested in and benefit from the systems they rage against. How we receive their anger will impact how available that anger is to them as a source of information, a barometer of injustice, and whether they can access it as motivation for creating something better.

Clearly we are talking about deeply emotional, resonant relationships. "I love these girls," Edell says of the SPARKteam. Program Coordinator Melissa Campbell agrees. "The girls are like super in my heart, they're a huge part of my life."

> They remind me so much of me when I was a teenager . . . like kind of angsty, kind of angry, wanting to do something, not really sure how to do it. I remember how difficult it was. I remember how easy it was to feel alone, like when you didn't have any real friends and things weren't fair, the way that the uncool kids were treated, kids who were perceived to be anything but straight were treated, or the way that girls who were loud or who took up space were treated, and you couldn't do anything about them.

These memories become a source of information, a way to experience common ground and shared motivation for doing the work together. Facilitating Sisters in Strength takes Amina Harris back to her adolescence too, and feeds her desire to be the "judgment-free" adult she once needed and didn't have.

> I'm not much older than they are, but I think that it was really hard for me to ask for help at their age; to not have it feel like, "Oh my gosh, I'm a basket case now," or "I'm a wreck." I have not had the best relationships with adults who were supposed to be in positions of support. Like my high school guidance counselor was terrible, like really terrible, and my teachers were terrible. So to be able to not be that, to be something different, is really, really important. I think that people make quick judgments about folks all the time based on preconceived notions about who a person might be or where it is that they're coming from."

Having experienced judgment as a girl means that Harris is always "checking where that comes from and, like, what sort of places in my life have I judged and how have people judged me and to really try to free myself from that and really be present for a person in that judgment-free zone."

Conversations with girls about such memories and shared experiences mean a lot, Alice says, especially when adults are "honest about [their] own adolescence" and "don't overlay [their] teenagehood onto girls" or "put [girls] on a pedestal: 'I wish I had been you as a girl.'" This means being honest with ourselves about what we want from girls, so that we don't project our stuff onto them—our needs in relationship, our wish for them to know what we know in the ways that we know it, our version of girlhood or success. If we've done our own work, if we can set aside our ego investment in whatever we are doing together, sharing memories can deepen our relationships and create space for girls to be who they are and imagine their own possibilities. "It's important not to try to live through the young people," Smith explains. "This is their time to be the young people, and your time to be the person that you are, in whatever stage you're in, and so be that." This means knowing and admitting what we don't know and respecting how age and all range of experiences make us different from girls.

For Campbell, working with girl activists at SPARK brings her back to what was not possible for her growing up white and in poverty.

My family was very poor and at one point in high school, I was considered technically homeless because we had lost our house and I was passing from place to place. And even though I was a person who thought there was injustice in the world, because I was living it, like I knew that all of these things were wrong, I was so much more concerned with getting to school and getting to work and graduating and never looking back, that activism was not a thing that I ever could have taken on, at any kind of scale.

Seeing "firsthand what it looks like when girls don't feel like I did when I was growing up" and what it feels like to have adults in their lives who say, "No, I get this, I get you; here's what we can do," has been motivating for Campbell. But knowing from her own experience that "if you're worried about whether or not you can pay your bills and if you're worried about whether or not you can eat, then [activism] isn't going to be your focus," drives her to go to "great lengths to make the SPARKteam accessible to girls who otherwise would not have anything like it."

> I knew that things were wrong in the world and the injustice of it kind of made me angry, but I had so many other things to worry about. Like, you are never going to start a feminist club at your school if you need to work every day after school, but you could do SPARK if you had to work every day after school, because we're much more flexible . . . and that's really, really important to me.

Such memories clarify "the difference our programs can make in girls' lives," Campbell says. They provide adults with motivation to offer constructive outlets for girls' anger and sense of injustice. They remind us why people who "get them" are so important.

To "get" girls, though, isn't all that easy. We have to pay attention; we have to be present and we have to listen actively. "The biggest mistake adults make is not listening to girls," Edell says. "I mean, as much as I say, 'Oh, we listen all the time,' it's really hard; we need to work at it all the time. Like, are we doing things without checking in with the girls first? Are we really hearing them or are we just hearing what we want to hear? Like really listening and actually considering what they're saying in a real way?"

Adults who really listen become acutely aware of the barriers girls face to their visible activism, not the least of which are the risks and potential dangers of open dissent. Edell worries about the "online hate" the SPARKteam gets when they blog about controversial issues and "the crap they take for speaking up and being feminists; the constant testing and pushback from both adults and peers" when they bring their activist leanings into their schools and communities. "There are definitely times when I worry about the girls, a lot," Edell says. "I kind of take that home with me, of like, Oh my god, what's going to happen, so-and-so got attacked in the media for this and is she going to be okay?"

It's a struggle to offer adult support that doesn't cross over to control and protection, especially when girls seem at risk of being hurt or misunderstood. It's hard not to override girls' voices by jumping in to protect them or deflect common stereotypes and misrepresentations. Girls who stand up, speak out, and take up space, Campbell says, "are called bossy, and bitchy, and loud, and all the awful things we call girls when they don't fit into these neat little boxes. It's difficult to be a real girl leader and activist today, because there are such narrow expectations for how girls are supposed to act."

As cochair of the Working Group on Girls at the United Nations, gender professor Emily Bent writes about the difficulty of supporting outspoken young radical feminists who refuse to "play the game." When Sierra, "an insightful sixteen-year-old South Korean girl living in the Bronx," known for her "bold ability to speak truth to power," drafts a list of best practices for adults who are "engaging girls in international panels, sessions, and meetings," Bent finds herself both completely supportive and also concerned with how Sierra's list will be received. Sierra pulls no punches. "Check your PhD at the door," she writes. "Your PhD, your job title, even your '50 years' experience working with girls' mean nothing here. . . . Also, no academic or policy-based jargon. . . . Meet us where we are." And by all means, she continues, "*Learn to listen.* I've facilitated panels with both adults and younger activists, and it's always the older 'experts' who like to go on and on, even sometimes ignoring cues to stop. Notice if you're talking too much, and stop."

But Sierra's most blunt, and perhaps most useful advice adds a new twist to a popular term: "*Don't momsplain.* Don't put words into our mouths. . . . I am not your daughter. I don't want your general, unsolicited advice on life, or false promises that things will get better as I get older. I want you to see me as a human being, and recognize that even if my status as a minor is not permanent, these issues will be unless we act."[2]

In the final analysis, our ability to work effectively with girls requires our full presence and our ability to embrace a balancing act—to live with some certainty in a precarious place. Personal and political touchstones—our girlhoods, unresolved feelings about power and authority, compromises we've felt pressed to make, the oppressions we've experienced and the hurts and losses we've endured, our explorations and understanding of power and privilege—offer information but not a clear way forward. We know all this and remain unsettled, at the mercy of the moment, in the service of what is required to enable the conditions for girls to challenge injustice.[3] As Megan Williams, who is white and president of Hardy Girls Healthy Women, says, our job is to be "the adults who are willing to not really lead the girls but stand with them, not tell girls how to do it, but support them as they figure it out. It's about meeting girls where they are and hearing their stories and trusting in their experiences and inspiring them to do their best work, instead of showing them how to do the kind of work you think they should be doing."

"The theory that we are all talking about is really, really complicated, complex, and personal, and dangerous," Dana Edell explains. The missing information, the unknown variable, is always the girls—what they bring. "And when we disagree with girls," Edell says, "I think that's an incredible challenge that happens . . . and I love the debate and we need both sides of it all the time, and we need to hear girls' perspectives. We just need to constantly raise awareness. We need to talk about it."

Making Room for Beautiful, Organic Things

When we let go of what we think we know, surprising, creative, and wonderful ideas emerge in activist work with girls. The result, says Jackie Dupont, who is white and Hardy Girls vice president of programs and research, is that "beautiful, organic things happen." Borders rise and fall and sometimes melt away, and moments of playfulness and fun sustain everyone through the hard work. Edell recalls her experience with the SPARKteam at a retreat. "We had this séance one night. Everyone's sleeping in this big crazy apartment in Chinatown, and it was a really funny moment. I felt like I was part of a summer campfire, and I didn't realize that I'm twenty years older than a lot of them. I just felt in it, with them as one of the girls." Dupont finds herself laughing at the absurd and funny parts of her own contradictions, something girls see and love to point out. "One of the things about the relationship with the [girls] is how smart and funny they are," she says. "They will literally have me in stitches, they're just so quick, so it reminds me that, 'Oh yeah, I can think that this is funny.'"

In these relational moments women are changed. "I've learned to continue to take risks, and to do my own work," Dupont says. We learn things. "When we're running campaigns, there are constantly little moments all the time where I'm like, 'Wow, that was really smart. Cool, I'm going to take that with me when I do something else,'" Edell says. But more than that, she adds, while working with girls whose "courage blows my mind, I have learned to be honest and brave."

> The way that girls just put themselves out there and talk about what they believe in, knowing that they're going to get harassed for it online, and also in their schools, and often in their families as well and so it's a huge risk for a lot of them to actually do this work. So I have so much respect for the courage and strength it takes them to do it. I learn to not care when the haters are going to hate. I learn from the girls to just brush it off and I have a supportive community and I'm a good person and let whatever happens happen. I learn how important it is to surround myself with people who support the work that I'm doing politically, and also personally and socially. I really see in them their hunger to

have feminist friends, and this makes me not take for granted my feminist friends and really see how valuable it is that I have a community of adults who I can go to when I need them.

For Campbell, too, being in relationship with girl activists has been deeply transformative: "Oh my God! To love things with the enthusiasm of a child, I think, is the most important thing. I've learned to just really feel things, throw myself into them. Let yourself mess up and trust in the support systems that are around you. I think that is the thing that they have taught me."

In my own work with girl activists, I know things are going well when girls can express strong feelings and stay in relationship, when we can disagree, when we can talk about our differences and still find our way through tough spots; when what's happening between us is, to use educator Amy Sullivan's language, "evocative." This, of course, is what genuine relationships are always like—a series of negotiations and compromises that require attention, reflection, and deep feeling; opportunities to work things out, risk new ideas, "speak the unspeakable and thus regain a sense of [our] own power."[4] For women partnering with girls, being real means letting girls know them, sharing experiences, inviting girls into their lives in ways that feel meaningful and useful. There are always parameters—responsibilities to appreciate, conditions to consider, systems to negotiate. But whatever the situation calls for, girls ask that we show up with all the parts of ourselves that make us knowledgeable, strong, and vulnerable, and with our hearts in the right place.

CHAPTER SIX

Experts on Their Own Experience

Respect for Girls' Knowledge

Alice was a high school sophomore when she first saw *Miss Representation*, a documentary about the unbalanced portrayal of women in the media and its impact on girls. While the movie inspired her to do a senior project on the Bechdel test,[1] she was a little disappointed in its overall message. "One thing that sort of frustrated me about *Miss Representation* was that the movie ends and it's basically like, well, everything's terrible; you know, sexualization is the worst, girls are in the worst position, The End. And I was like, wait, are you not going to tell us what to do about it?"

Alice was not new to protests. She grew up attending political marches and rallies, first with her parents and then on her own. "But it always felt like something that was organized by adults and it was like, you know, you could attend and have a sign, and since you were a kid they would take pictures of you, because it's like, 'Oh a child holding a sign for something. It's a good photo op.'" But her participation in SPARK was different. "SPARK was a lot more radical. As opposed to telling us, like, here are your options, like, 'Okay, let's give this kid a couple of things to get her excited about democracy,' SPARK was actually asking us what we wanted to do about it." Alice says it "had an impact on me" when

Dana Edell, SPARK's executive director, told the girls at the outset, "'You are the expert on your own experiences.' Like, no one had ever really said that to me before."

Alice, seventeen, knows she risks sounding "really cynical," but in truth, she adds, "All you are really allowed to do as a teenager is complain about things. So when somebody comes to you and says, like, 'Hey, we're gonna give you the tools to make things better,' and tells you that your experiences matter, it's just . . . so inspiring and, you know, empowering." So empowering that she had, as a result, "this epiphany that I deserve better then what's happening currently," that she had a right to claim the authority of her experiences of injustice and a responsibility to use them to demand a better world.

The girls say repeatedly how powerful it is when adults see them as experts and trust them as guides. They appreciate adults who acknowledge, as Simone, seventeen and a GAB member, says, "that the world has changed since when they were teenagers, and so teenagers know what they're fighting and they know what it's like to be in school, to be in society as a teenager." As Edell says, girls "can actually talk about being a teenage girl more than I can." Adults who really listen understand that girls have a reason for "doing something different than what [adults] would think," Simone says, and they trust, adds fifteen-year-old Lily, that girls aren't dupes: "We know what we're getting into. We know what we're talking about. We don't just hear something and think it's cool." We offer "different perspectives," Sam, eighteen, agrees. The girls value those adults who "know we know," says nineteen-year-old Celeste, who advises, "Don't underestimate girls. Girls are way smarter than [you] think they are. . . . Girls have insights into oppression adults may not experience."

Really listening to girls in her work at Girls for Gender Equity, Joanne Smith says, requires her, and all of us as adults, to "stretch ourselves and understand it's their time now, and while we still have the same issues, we have to be open to different strategies for addressing them." These strategies emerge when we "let girls take the reins," adds Darla Linville, who is white and an education professor at Augusta University in Georgia and who, as a member of the Public Science Project at City University of New York, developed participatory action projects with queer youth as a way to understand their experiences in schools. This means giving them ownership, a sense that this is "their time . . . their space." SPARK's Melissa Campbell agrees. "It's important that the SPARK girls are at the forefront, because they are the ones who know what it's like living in this world as girls and young women." Campbell, who at twenty-four is not much older than the young women she works with, adds, "I have a pretty good recollection of what it was like being a teenager, but that was five years ago now and so much has changed in five years."

It's not easy for adults to stretch ourselves in this way, much less to hand over the reins. It's difficult not to assume our way is better or that what we know is naturally superior to anything a girl offers. But, as eighteen-year-old SPARKteam member Katy says, it's important that adults break away from "doing things like they've always done them." Hardy Girls president Megan Williams wants the college students who run the nonprofit's activist groups with younger girls to know how important it is to question what "we're so trained" to assume, "that we have experience and knowledge that we just need to impart to them. It's so much more about meeting girls where they are and hearing their stories and trusting in their experiences and inspiring them to do their best work, instead of showing them how to do the kind of work you think they should be doing."

All of the women activists are passionate about this point. As adults working with girls, and with youth in general, we have to check our need to be right, to patrol the boundaries around the work we do together. We have to fight our impulse to "correct how young people have it wrong," Linville says, "or to tell them, you know, 'That's too idealistic.' 'That's not how the world works.' 'When you get a little older you'll understand.' In doing this kind of work, our role is not to be in that position with young people."

Knowing things, offering expertise, asking questions—these are different from controlling things, she explains:

> So we have a role as experts in some things, like I know how to do research. I can show you how to do this, right? These are some skills and some experiences I have and I can share them with you, but my role is not to tell you what is right on this issue. Because you are the expert, you have the experience, you're in it right now; you can tell me what's happening. You are the expert on this, so I'm not going to tell you that your experience is wrong or your perception is wrong.

The girls talk about how freeing it is to work with adults who have such faith in them, who, when given the option, choose "to run toward girls," in the words of sixteen-year-old Amber, a youth organizer with Sisters in Strength. They know the difference between being invited in by an adult and being "boxed in by her as an authoritarian," says GAB member Treva, eighteen. And many know all too well what it means to be a token girl in an adult-driven project, something sixteen-year-old Yas says she's had plenty of experience with.

> There is one organization I worked with, I was in the group but I felt like everything, all the decisions, were being made by the adults. I felt like they sort of, they wanted me there because I was a young person and because they wanted a young person's opinion. But they ultimately wanted it to be about what they wanted. And I guess I felt like a lot of the time they would come up with things they wanted me to do rather than me coming up with the ideas myself. And they would ask me to do them. Um, but I didn't actually do it.

Sociologist Roger Hart developed a useful model of children's participation some years ago for UNICEF.[2] Each rung of his "ladder of participation" represents the nature of children's engagement

with adults in community and organizational projects. The lowest
rungs represent the kind of tokenism Yas refers to and the highest
depict youth-initiated projects and negotiated partnerships with
adults. If adults experience girls' resistance or their disappearance
in key moments, they can assume girls, like Yas, are not invested
for a reason. "[We] aren't just like mere figureheads," Katy insists.
If girls are going to work with adults we want to "lead initiatives of
[our] own," and, as SIS member Cheyanne says, tackle "everyday
issues relevant to [our] lives." We want to "bring our own ideas, to
bring what we have to the table," GAB member Lily agrees. Alice
refers to this way of centering girls' experiences and knowledge as
girl-driven activism, which means, she says, "We really are in the
driver's seat or at the very least in the passenger's seat. Like, the
girls ultimately are the ones who are in control."

The tension in this description is real—it's not easy to switch
from driver to passenger and back again; it takes a lot of trust in
the other person. In intergenerational girl-driven activist projects
girls bring their expertise, initiate projects, and drive momentum;
they determine the pace when the road twists and turns. Yet when
they find themselves at critical intersections, they can rely on experienced, trustworthy adults for advice or support before choosing
which way to turn. It's in those moments of negotiation that so
much can happen—where girls can slip easily into the passenger's
seat or a struggle for the wheel can stop the car altogether. The
key to SPARK's girl-centered way of working, says Dana Edell, is
that "girls' voices, experiences, writing, and ideas are really at the
forefront" in these moments, "not the adults so much." At Girls
for Gender Equity, Amina Harris says, adults enable the conditions that "allow [girls] to bring their lived experiences, to create
the systems and the solutions to some of these problems." In her
feminist classroom where students develop activist projects, Ileana
Jiménez believes it is critically important that students' "actions
and projects come from a really authentic place."

Adults who enable girl-driven activism ask questions, Hardy
Girls' Megan Williams says, like "What is it that you want to do

about this?" and "Where would you like to take this?" They create the space for girls to explore and think and identify problems and help them connect their individual experiences with shared experiences. "And then, once they want to do something about it," Williams adds, "we help them think about what change they want to effect, and how they might do that." Girls acknowledge and appreciate such space and support, but they don't always see or recognize women activists' struggle with the tension between trusting what girls know and offering advice. "It's about finding a good balance," says SPARK's Melissa Campbell, "because you don't want to be totally hands-off, because you are there for a reason, but then you don't want to be directing the conversation too much. So your voice should not be a leading voice, it should be a gentle guiding voice."

Letting go in this gentle, thoughtful way is a challenge, in part because it does involve looking closely at and unlearning what we think we know about girls and about working with youth. For Campbell, Williams, and other women activists, this means listening carefully and trusting the girls in front of us, the relationships we have with them, not the stereotypes and stock phrases used to describe youth, and girls in particular. Williams explains:

> I think that there's a real misconception from an adult point of view about what kids are capable of and what they want to do, and the idea that kids don't care about things these days and all they want to do is get on their Tumblr or Instagram or whatever, and girls are so mean and they can't trust one another, and all they want to do is fight with one another. And there are these stereotypes that adults have or construct or learn about girls that simply aren't true, but they are very much widely accepted in our culture and society, and so I think that's one of the biggest barriers.

These assumptions can cause adults to hold tight, to over-control for fear that girls won't follow through or that they will overreact and make a relational mess of things. And while girls are almost always better able to tackle things than we expect, Jackie Dupont says, thinking back to her work on the Girls Advisory Board at Hardy Girls, there are consequences to letting go. "You have to kind of be OK with things not going according to plan, and things being done last minute." But there's no other way. If we trust in girls, if we believe in what they are capable of, and if we believe the real benefits of this work come from the doing of it, we need to step back and allow them to drive. "I have to remind myself periodically that they are getting it done," Dupont says, "and not to be constantly harassing them to tell me exactly where they are and not to freak out." She continues:

> This is one of the first opportunities that girls have to be leaders, to control, have control over a situation, and it is going to be messy because they haven't had practice before. You get used to it and you have plan C and D. So that's where adults have to do their own work. I am challenged not to take over a project and to do things for them, and that may mean that I watch them fail beautifully, and that's hard. So that's a challenge, it's a challenge to let go.

There are moments for adults to offer a big-picture view of possibilities and consequences, to provide guidance and share useful information or expertise, but offering these things upfront as things to consider in the brainstorming and planning process, and then additional support when asked, ensures girls have opportunities to problem-solve and gives them a sense of ownership. When it all works, when girls have, in Treva's words, "authority to make decisions instead of it being run by adults," the results are transformative. "Asking us what we want to do," Alice says, "as opposed to telling us gives girls creative power." Simone concurs that the space to consider and choose "helps us figure out what we care about." Everyone is changed when adults have faith "that girls can play a role in shaping the movement," Smith says, when we all believe, as Jiménez believes of her students, "that they could be pioneers."

Why Not Me?

For Alice, who is white, this transformation has been huge. When she joined the SPARKteam, she found it was hard to let go of the usual vertical ways of working with adults and within systems because she had little past experience with "open lines of communication and trust," and so little opportunity to offer her ideas and be taken seriously. She came to see how much a risk-averse education system obsessed with individual success and high-stakes testing had limited her. "You just kind of do what you need to do. You don't get in trouble. And there is this constant fear of 'I'm going to get fired or kicked out if I do this.'" It's hard to take chances when the punishment for mistakes or the risk of misstep is so high. To Alice, it feels like "everything is all like consequences for us. Like, if you don't get this score on this exam, you're just gonna be a failure." If creative activism is going to thrive, Alice thinks girls and adults together have to consciously address and disrupt a system that rewards safety and conformity:

> I think it's important to expel that right from the start and take away that kind of fear so that people feel comfortable taking chances and having big ideas and failing. And making that OK. Like, failure is important. That's not a new idea, but to make sure people feel comfortable with that, and have open lines of communication with adults—and also feel like, feel really safe with them.

These open lines of communication with adults who take girls seriously are "powerful" for Alice because they invite "big ideas" in response to injustice. Alice recalls how "distraught" she and the other girls on the SPARKteam felt in response to the 2012 rape of a sixteen-year-old girl by a group of football players in Steubenville,

Ohio, and how important it was to talk with adult activists and mobilize together around their strong reactions.[3] The "painful" reality that this could have been any one of them incited enormous energy among the girls to "do something about it."

> It started out with all of us, like, talking and saying, "OK we're all really upset and angry. Let's talk about how we want to translate this anger into action." And it felt like, oh, this is the kind of thing that, yeah, like you don't just have to be outraged, you can do something with that. We can do more than just talk about how horrified we are that this happened. We could actually do something about it, and you know, possibly prevent that kind of thing from happening again.

The girls' conversations were predicated on a belief in their agency—their capacity to use what they know from their own experiences to imagine creative solutions and to transform thoughts and strong emotions into meaningful action. The girls were struck by the football players' privileged status among their peers and especially the Steubenville coach's ardent defense of the boys involved, something many had experienced or could imagine in their own high schools. They wondered what training the coaches receive about sexual-violence prevention, and with a little research were shocked to discover that the National Federation of State High School Associations (NFHS), an organization that trains high school athletic coaches across the country, offered no educational materials or training on the issue.

It seemed to everyone—adults and girls—that SPARK needed to reach out to NFHS in a way that conveyed the girls' compassion for the victim in the Steubenville case and their fear that, without education and prevention strategies, something similar could happen in their schools. They brought together former SPARK-team member Carmen Rios and Colby College football player Connor Clancy, both involved in sexual-violence-prevention activism.[4] With support from SPARK and Shelby Knox, in her role as women's rights organizer at Change.org, Rios and Clancy petitioned NFHS to remedy this situation. At the same time, SPARK girls and adults researched and contacted organizations dedicated to sexual-violence prevention to ask for their engagement and endorsement. In the end, a coalition of state and national organizations agreed to work together to develop educational materials and easy access to sexual-violence-prevention resources for the nearly one hundred thousand high school coaches who seek out NFHS training materials.[5]

This was a powerful experience for Alice, not only because she was able to move from such intense emotion to take part in a strategic set of actions, but because of the scope of the project and the number of people affected. Something shifted in her and it felt seismic. "Oh, man. Oh, God," she says, describing the change from someone who felt little impulse to act in response to injustice— "that was not part of my routine"—to someone who now feels "an instinct to say, like, 'Oh, we should organize a protest!' You know, there is this kind of feeling that, like, Oh, why don't we just take care of this, write a blog, tweet about it, or take some kind of action around it instead of just sitting around and complaining about it." This is the kind of empowerment Alice describes in the opening of this chapter—a realization that her voice, her experiences, could change things. This is when "Why me?" she says, became "Why not me?"

The Radical Side of Trust

Respecting girls' knowledge and experience and inciting (rather than dismissing or dampening) their strong feelings, sense of urgency, and imagination requires, Dana Edell says, a way of working where "deep trust and respect for girls is the core." We build trust when we're willing to "help the girls navigate through [the system], to respect the choices they're making, to acknowledge that they have the right, of course, and that they own the choices they're making." We affirm that trust when we're brave enough to do what we can to "break apart" the systems that constrain what's possible for youth and when we face the consequences of our actions together. "We have to trust each other," Edell asserts.

> But that's actually really, really hard in practice, and I think for a lot of adults it's pretty radical, because we don't trust girls. We don't trust young people in this world, at all. Our entire education system, our entire capitalist system, our entire democracy basically, is based on the fact that if you're under eighteen, who cares? That you're not valuable, your opinions don't matter, you don't know your own life. You can't participate in our community. There are all of these things that they can't do.

The radical side of trust demands our willingness to interrupt the usual flow of power. When Darla Linville began her work with queer youth in New York City, she strove to create a relational environment that honored youth knowledge and expertise.[6] "I wanted to talk to them about being LGBTQ youth in the city and what experiences they were having in schools, what messages they were getting," Linville says. She imagined the group would do research together, but soon realized that honoring their expertise meant letting go of her way of working and allowing them ownership of the process. This meant adjusting her assumptions, even about what she initially considered the "distraction" of joking around. "I thought of the group as more research-focused. The demand from the students that there be a social aspect was really surprising to me, and oh my gosh. Some of those meetings just got so loud and rowdy and crazy."

> It was hard not to just jump in and react. It felt like the social was a little bit of a distraction because what we were talking about was hard and painful, because it was challenging, or people were going to say things that were maybe hard for them personally or would be hard for the group to hear. Then it became, "Hey let's goof off." But it just occurred to me that some of the most

insightful comments came out of the joking around. So you can't just tune out or just override the joking around because sometimes that is where a key gem of information comes out; [they're] trying to bring attention to something that they couldn't bring up in a serious way.

Linville's willingness to step back, to trust that the youth in her project know more about what they need to do the work that matters to them than she does, that they have a different understanding of process, is an act of faith. There's some truth to the adage "give an inch and they take a mile," but we so rarely acknowledge mile-taking as a source of new knowledge. Once freed from the usual barriers and the me/them binary, Linville says, the group engaged in "ongoing conversation about power in our research group," and settled in a place where "the young people had a lot of leadership in the group, especially in terms of saying, 'Yes this is a good idea,' 'Yes this is the right direction,' or 'No this isn't going to work,' 'We need to rethink this,' 'This doesn't make sense.'"

When we work through assumptions about what girls know, when we validate their experience and allow them to initiate actions, we discover qualities rarely acknowledged in any general or public way. "Girls have a lot of strength," Jackie Dupont says, reflecting on her work at Hardy Girls. "They have a way of seeing the world that can be very profound and creative and surprising. Every girl in every situation has strengths that can be built upon, and we can learn from girls as much as they learn from us." Unfettered or contained by assumptions about girls, Joanne Smith appreciates how "girls play such an important role" in the creative process of activism at Girls for Gender Equity, how they bring "fresh perspectives," how they "inspire" and "ignite" campaigns. It's the top-down or vertical relationships adults typically offer that's often the problem, not the girls.

Linville agrees. "They're full of passion and energy and creativity. They have so much to give. . . . They are questioning everything." And yet there is so much pressure on them not to know what they know, not to say what they feel and think. "In this modern moment, their voices are so silenced. They are given grief for even knowing themselves, much less knowing what is going on in the world. You know, they are called irresponsible and reckless and selfish and they are so clamped down on from every side that I think when you give them space to talk, it's just amazing."

Working with girls in a more horizontal, unbounded way can be eye-opening and expansive if we can let go of our need to defend our version of reality; if we don't "lead out of fear," Smith says, "or make decisions out of fear."

> The reality is that young people are making decisions for themselves a thousand times a day. I mean, from big to little, and your job is to be the adult, and at the same time create space and create the conditions for that young person to flourish. Part of that is having a reciprocal dialogue, offering support and compromising on some areas even when your fear is activated. Part of that is not always being the one talking, and doing more listening, and allowing that person to also guide the way.

Doing the reflective work to open space for girls' knowledge and expertise has as powerful an impact on adults as it does on girls. "I started Girls for Gender Equity thinking I was going to free our girls and save them and lead them in a way that I wish I had [been] when I was younger," Smith says. "And the reality is that they've freed me and continue to be the best gift to me." Linville laughs as she reflects on her intergenerational research project. "Oh, I've learned all of the ways that I don't meet my expectations. We are all one big disappointment." Her laughter suddenly turns serious as she considers the opportunity for personal growth in this work.

> You have to believe in the worth and value of what young people are saying. You have to believe that they have their own knowledge, which is not the same as the knowledge that you have given

them in your interactions with them. And that their knowledge might contradict yours. And be willing to listen to that. Not just talk over it or correct it. Be willing to be transformed.

It's a humbling experience, this realization that girls know things we don't and that relationships with girls can change who we are as adults. This is so far from what we have been taught to expect. It's easy to miss because we are buried in the adult version of things; we have assimilated to a narrow model of what such relationships with youth are or could be. Linville talks about how a different way of working with youth, one that respects their knowledge and centers their expertise, is so important for adult activists—how it opens us up and reminds us of what matters:

High schoolers, I think, are at this beautiful stage in their lives where they can still see the world very clearly, where they have not been completely convinced by the social structures, social niceties, that we as adults conform to. And they can still speak very clearly the truth about injustices and unfairness in the world. And they have a very strong sense, developmentally, of right and wrong and fair and unfair. And so I think that they are in this moment where they have a very clear-eyed vision and they can remind us as adults of the places where we have made compromises for social lubrication purposes [and] that sometimes those compromises are not in the interest of justice, and so we should rethink our stances sometimes. We should take up the fight again, and teenagers are good at reminding us about that.

It's through such relational transformations that adults become witnesses for girls, advocates for their perspectives and their right to be seen as experts on their own experience. When people contact Edell saying, "We want you to come talk about teenage girls," the SPARK executive director responds, "Actually, I have teenage girls who can talk about teenage girls." This is the goal, Smith agrees. At Girls for Gender Equity, "girls are the ones who do the research, the interviews; they are the ones who shape the questions and develop the language to gather up from other young people how it is our campaign needs to be shaped and how they can lift up stories from young people so that it further informs our campaign." So, of course, "they are the ones who testify to the Department of Education, to the United Nations. They're the ones on television, on [the MSNBC commentary program] *Melissa Harris-Perry*, in the film *Anita: Speaking Truth to Power*—the ones that are speaking from *their* experience, from *their* lens, on behalf of *their* peers."

"Our responsibility is to be the kind of trustworthy adult," Megan Williams says, "who is willing to stand with girls and support them and trust their decisions, and not just say that we trust them but also behave that way, which can be hard." It's hard to sit with girls as they struggle with ideas and decisions, it's hard to give up control when they challenge our process, it's uncomfortable to shift gears and to disrupt the way things usually go. But if we respect girls' knowledge, we also have to believe in their right to speak for themselves about issues that matter to them, and then we are obligated to support that right.

CHAPTER SEVEN

Wide Awake and Calling BS

Critical Consciousness

"Thinking critically is at the heart of anybody transforming their life," bell hooks writes, and "the heartbeat of critical thinking is the longing to know."[1] For the girls in this book, activist spaces are, by definition, opportunities to satisfy that longing. Such spaces are infused with what hooks calls "radical openness"—a frame of mind guided by imagination, never settling for the superficial, always biting at the heels of the status quo.[2] At their best, they are places of possibility, where "ambitions, desires, and real hope" for a more just world thrive.[3]

Critique and possibility drive Ileana Jiménez's activist work with students. In her high school course on feminism and activism, Jiménez guides her students, both girls and boys, "through the process of understanding theory and what it is used for," and encourages them to be "reflective" and "close readers" of the texts she assigns. Through teaching women-of-color feminism, reading a range of texts together "from Audre Lorde to bell hooks to Angela Davis and more," she asks students to understand how feminist theory can be used to examine their own lives, which are "inherently intersectional," moving them to grapple with how "gender connects to and intersects with race, class, sexuality, ethnicity, politics, and human rights." As a "feminist queer teacher of color," Jiménez shares her own stories with students about how she "navigates both systems of oppression and privilege" and helps her students "examine their stories so that they can see how they also both contribute to and benefit from systems of oppression." And as an activist, Jiménez creates opportunities for her students to extend that capacity for reflection and critique to the situations and systems they inhabit.

This pairing of critical thinking and social awareness, leading to what Brazilian educational theorist Paulo Freire called *conscientização*, or critical consciousness, is at the heart of Jiménez's practice.[4] "I try to have my students think about the things they go through every day that actually affect them," she says. Her goal is to create the conditions for her students to recognize injustice in their world and feel moved to do something about it. Everything hinges on "asking students to make it more personal." Jiménez explains: "How does that apply to you? I think that the move to applying it to your own life and then sharing that sort of testimony and personal storytelling allows for the next step to happen, which is the activism piece." She provides her students with opportunities to feel, to experience, "to understand each other as individuals and understand their position within systems" by taking them to activist events, connecting them to causes.

> So if their passion is the environment, then I would ask them to learn about immigration rights and how that connects to the environment. And if their passion is the sexualization of women and girls in media, I would ask them to look at how that connects to domestic sex-trafficking. I would ask them to look at multi-issues, so that they see not just their own passionate issue, but how it connects to other issues. And then they can do the work much more thoughtfully.

Jiménez invites activists into her classroom, who open up these connections and challenge her students' taken-for-granted views, and every year she and her class of juniors and seniors put together an International Day of the Girl assembly for the entire student body. Jiménez describes this as "an intersectional feminist intervention," because the students deliberately make a connection between global and local injustices affecting girls and women. She describes last year's event as particularly powerful for her students, who chose to connect barriers to girls' education in the Global South to barriers girls of color experience right in their own communities. Some of the girls in her class put together a presentation using statistics and findings from the Black Lives Matter movement and the African American Policy Forum report *Say Her Name*, which documents the invisible violence experienced by girls and women of color at the hands of police.[5] Jiménez explains: "Many students in the room know the names of Eric Garner and Trayvon Martin, but when [my students] read the names of girls and women of color who have been killed and murdered at the hands of police brutality and other forms of violence against women of color, not many hands went up because those names are not known and recognized. There's an erasure, an invisibility around violence against women of color." The students then shared stories about "being harassed at school or at parties, or in public spaces such as the subway or cabs," Jiménez says. "And one girl shared a story about how she had hailed a cab to go to school and the man was basically harassing her and asking inappropriate questions the entire time she was in the cab and she felt very trapped and scared."

> She wound up sharing that story not only at the assembly but also at a local feminist bookstore in New York City for a street-harassment event led by Holly Kearl, who had just written a book about global street harassment. My student said she felt that much more empowered to share her story not only to her peers at school but also to a larger public audience. It's in those moments that the personal becomes political and has a greater impact in creating solidarity and action with others.

The assembly was a powerful intervention. The impact of the girls' stories of harassment in public spaces inspired a group of girls who had taken Jiménez's class the previous year to approach her about starting a feminist club. It was their senior year and they wanted to bring the issues home, so to speak, by addressing harassment they experienced in the school. Their first target was the school dress code, which, as Jiménez explains, "was not addressing all of the ways they felt like they were being targeted." They wanted "a more intersectional revision of the dress code," she says, "and so they began to revise it with the lens of keeping girls of color in mind and the fact that we had at least one transgender girl in the school. They wanted a trans-inclusive, anti-racist dress code." The girls developed a new version of the dress code and, with behind-the-scenes support from Jiménez, presented it to the faculty.

> They explained how the current dress code relates to a larger slut-shaming culture, a larger rape culture, a culture of sexual harassment, and it really started a conversation with the faculty. The faculty had a real moment where they thought, "Wait, maybe we should be looking at our own internalized messages, our own notions of sexism, and our own internalized misogyny." It wasn't across the board, but there were definitely moments when faculty started to do their own interior work near the end of that conversation.

Jiménez describes the moment her students grasp the activist power of storytelling as "the breaking point"—a shift in thinking, in perspective, powerful enough to transform their way of being in the world. "I think that is probably the most important thing in this whole work," she says, "which is not only how you scaffold girls' activist work, but primarily have them find a voice to do that activism."

Ileana Jiménez teaches in a progressive private school. Her administration is supportive, even proud, of the work she does. She knows her situation is not the norm, far from it. But she believes there are feminist teachers in all kinds of schools and classrooms across the country developing critical consciousness in their students. So when she's not teaching, Jiménez is developing her blog, *Feminist Teacher*, into "a place of community and conversation"; a place for other k–12 feminist educators to learn and connect. Her goal, she writes, "is to make us visible to each other and to the larger world of educators, as we move forward with our important work."[6]

The Social Is Political

It perhaps goes without saying, then, that critical consciousness emerges out of experiences of relationship. "As we learn about activism, we also learn about each other," says sixteen-year-old Sisters in Strength member Jasmine—and, as Ileana Jiménez's class suggests, vice versa. "It all ties together." It requires someone willing to interrupt "the way things are"[7]—to ask genuine questions, call attention to contradictions, reveal larger patterns, and stay with us as we grapple with difficult consequences. This all matters. Before we can hope to imagine new possibilities or replace old injustices, we need to thoughtfully examine what's right in front of us.

Critical consciousness, in this sense, "is a way of being as well as a way of thinking, a relation to others as well as an intellectual capacity."[8] It's a social activity. It's a function of being together; a way of challenging one another. It's where we take up feminist scholar Chandra Mohanty's call to create "public cultures of dissent."[9] Spaces that invite critical consciousness are marked by diversity. The girls and women know from experience what Gloria Steinem attests: "We learn from difference, not from sameness."[10] Difference offers the possibility of thinking otherwise. "Criticality is a practice, a mark of what we do, of who we are, and not only how we think."[11] SPARK projects in which Izzy, a white fifteen-year-old from Maine, and Celeste, a nineteen-year-old Mexican American from California, team up with "girls of different cultural backgrounds," all bringing, Celeste says, "our own experiences to the forefront," create possibilities for genuine discussion and learning. Supporting and engaging a diversity of opinion is "radical," SPARKteam's Alice explains. "Having all these girls from all over the world in their different environments talking about these things" is the best hope for effective solutions to problems.

Intergenerational spaces are marked by differences in perspective and experience. On the SPARK Movement, Hardy Girls, and *Powered by Girl* private Facebook groups where girls talk and plan with adults, girls will often ask for help understanding and responding to troubling situations that they or their friends find themselves in. What should they do when boys at their school are supporting and sharing a slut-shaming Instagram account? How do they talk with a teacher who consistently ridicules their feminism in front of other students? How do they help a friend who says she was sexually assaulted? Each question is an invitation to consider possibilities, to see things in a broader light, to imagine creative solutions together.

When I ask Alice, who is white and middle class, how the adults in SPARK have helped her think more deeply about issues, she tells me a story: "In high school a friend asked me, 'What do you think about weight? I know we are all body positive, but isn't it unhealthy?' And I was like, 'I don't even know the answer.' So I texted Melissa [Campbell, SPARK's programs coordinator], and I was like, 'So, what is it? I'm not sure how to answer this question. I don't feel like I know enough.'" Alice wasn't sure what she wanted from Melissa, maybe some health advice, maybe some body-acceptance websites, so she was completely surprised when Melissa asked her to think about the relationship between weight and poverty: "She sent me this article and a long response about how, like, in city planning there aren't sidewalks and how there aren't public parks and stuff where people can go and exercise and stuff, and if it's a dangerous neighborhood, like you're going to stay inside your house and you're not going to go for a run with your dog."

Alice hadn't considered that "wealthier people have access to greenways, parks, and access to gyms," or how "in city planning, that it's all about cars, not about biking or walking anywhere." Connecting the dots, Alice said, "just, like, totally blew my mind." She began to think about how circumstances affect people's lives in profound ways. "And it's just so powerful to be like, Oh, OK, so it's actually like some white girl down the street will get arrested for pot and nothing will happen to her. She'll just be back in high school the next day smoking weed in the parking lot. But if that was a black kid they would be in jail, and suddenly you know that and you're like, oh my God, and it just changes your whole world."

For Melissa to extend a simple question—"What do you think about weight?" to an examination of power and privilege introduces Alice to a new habit of mind, which is to cultivate a healthy suspicion of simple, surface explanations and to read situations for inequities. Other girls describe similar experiences. "We have open discussions among each other and [adults] urge us to think critically about different topics, different things that we are learning about so we can fully understand it," Sisters in Strength member Cheyanne, sixteen, says. It's the "It just changes your world" moment that Ileana Jiménez works toward and that so energizes Alice, and it's the company, the shared support, and the shared realization of injustice that motivates Amber, also sixteen and a Sisters in Strength member, to believe that "whatever we learn we need to take it back to the school, to our everyday lives."

It's powerful, SPARKteam member Maya, a white nineteen-year-old, says, "to talk about what we see and what makes us angry, and then try to figure out how to change it." It's having the permission to feel and talk that's so important. Unsurprisingly, girls say, there are few spaces in their everyday lives where they are encouraged to process what they experience, to express strong feelings, to ask and sit with unsettling questions. For middle and high school girls working through their complicated relationships with peers, teachers, and parents, such disruptions are risky in lots of ways, so activist spaces might be the only opportunity they have to develop these new habits of thought, a rare opportunity to build a language and develop ideas that challenge the barriers they experience. "Kids around my age are going through struggles, are facing problems like, you know, gender-based violence or sexual harassment, things like that," Amber says. "So, you know . . . it's helped me and I feel like it expands my mind on different things to be aware of."

The girls talk about the power of revelation, as what seemed simple or everyday life opens up to them in new and surprising ways. This revelation invites a desire to dig deep and probe issues—to explore our doubts, to know what we don't yet know, to name what limits and oppresses, what obscures and distracts. In her work with the Girls Advisory Board at Hardy Girls, Megan Williams, like Ileana Jiménez, provides opportunities through discussion and storytelling for girls "to see patterns of oppression and begin to name things as unfair and connect them to the bigger systems at play." Naming is a process of seeing to the bottom, of uncovering the underlying causes and effects.

The women activists talk about how they support this shift to naming the deeper processes at work. They ask questions, expose contradictions, and create opportunities to look more closely at what's in front of them. In her work with queer youth from public high schools in New York City, Darla Linville talks about how she created opportunities to examine the homophobia she and they experienced daily.

I brought in copies of things like reports and newspaper articles . . . and we just broke off into groups of two and took highlighters and said, you know, "What are the important statements being made here?" And we wrote them up on a whiteboard and we talked about whose interest, whose point of view, who wins and who loses when things are said this way. What is supposed to be the "right" way to think about this? What are different ways to look at this? So how can we reframe it? And then what is our own point of view of what is right and what is wrong in terms of gender nonconformity in schools? What are these points of view and what are the claims, the aims, the politics, the power or the interests of these different points of view, and then what's our own? How are we seduced or caught up in using this kind of language? But then, how do we make our own framework for how we are going to think about this? So, really teasing that all apart and then labeling it and deciding where we stand within it.

Question after question, inviting scrutiny and evaluation of what appears on the surface to be clear and certain, Linville says, was "really, really essential because when we started talking, the only language we had to talk about it were the things that kids were hearing at school or the behaviors that kids were seeing in schools or the interactions they were having with peers or teachers. The only way we had to talk about it was within those other frameworks."

Understanding the "seduction" of prevailing points of view; naming "the claims, the aims, the politics, the power . . . the interests" that push their realities to the margins, erase them, or make them problematic, opens up space for youth to challenge these "truths" with their own experiences. This is essential work and, as Ileana Jiménez says, "intentional" work. "I think the biggest challenge is trying to distill these really huge concepts of systemic, systems of oppression, and bring in real lived experiences and to connect all the dots," Amina Harris says of her work with the girls in Sisters in Strength. This requires "giv[ing] fundamental background knowledge and foundational understanding," yes, but also allowing "the learning to happen organically, experientially, and to have it really be driven by the action" that arises from it.

"I think those of us who work in social justice see so many gaps, and absences, and moments for things to be addressed," Jiménez says. When adults cultivate the art of noticing the absences, asking questions, and posing alternatives, they invite girls to do the same. Izzy talks about how much it matters to her when adults "don't tell me that what I'm doing is a bad idea or a really good one," but "just tell me, like, 'Look to yourself. What do you think it is?'" In Izzy's words, such people teach her "how to open my mind to new ideas and how to find out within myself how to do other things. . . . I like the independence and freedom." For her fellow GAB member Treva, it's the "things that we see and parts of everyday life" that make such questions and conversations personally valuable and meaningful.

Grappling with hard conversations about differences, examining together the ways power and privilege play out in their work together, is fundamental to activist practice. Girls say such questions facilitate deeper discussions and encourage them to take their analysis into the world. "Whenever something comes up, when there's an issue or something that makes us mad or there's a problem," SPARKteam member Julia says, "the adults bring to that conversation like, 'What's wrong? What do you think? Why are you so mad about this one thing?' Because often we just complain and say, 'Oh it just makes me so mad.' But to stop and think why, like, what's wrong with it?" It's this challenge to think about, "to have a more in-depth discussion about that topic," GAB member Cassidy says, that encourages the girls to take their thoughts and feelings seriously—to move them into the public realm. Just as Jiménez urges the youth she teaches to take their personal stories and turn them into testimonies, "not staying within the self, but moving outward into the world."

Becoming the Person You Want to Be

It's powerful, Alice says, when adults say to girls, "OK, we're really upset and angry right now. How do we want to translate this anger into action? We can do more than just talk, [we can] impact people's lives." It's also risky. Challenging the taken-for-granted is unsettling, even scary. It affects how girls relate to their friends, to their families, how they experience school and community. It's important to do the relational work, then, that "dispels fear of failure from the start," Alice says, so people can "take chances," or as Cheyanne says, "expand their views." Girls want environments that, in Amber's words, "push to the source of the problem." They want people, Celeste says, who "challenge norms and step up and into hard conversations." But they also need people who take the time to talk about the implications of their decisions and who help them gauge the dangers. As Hardy Girls' Megan Williams says, "We have to have laid the groundwork for girls to feel like they have the critical consciousness to both name what's wrong and to have the agency to say, 'I can do something about this,' and also have the support available to say with confidence, 'I know that I have people behind me in this.'"

The girls talk a lot about the ways coming to critical consciousness changes all aspects of their lives. Learning to question and look more closely at what's happening around her led sixteen-year-old Brianna, a member of Sisters in Strength's youth-organizing program, to take a new interest in her school's Bill of Rights. Rather than toss it aside with the other forms in her beginning-of-school-year packet, she and her friends repeated a process they learned in SIS—they "sat down at lunch analyzing and highlighting." Brianna became more aware of what she was asked to sign each year, what the school promised and didn't deliver, and how this affected her friends and classmates. "A lot of us thought it was just an everyday thing . . . we never really thought that there was anything we could do." She began to ask critical questions. Why wasn't this document presented clearly to students by the school administration? Why didn't students know their rights? Brianna pressed for answers and, unsatisfied, finally decided to act. She gave a "speech about school push-out, educating adults and classmates about the issue." Her friend and fellow Sisters in Strength member, Jasmine, was there to support her.

Simone, who is white, says that being part of the Girls Advisory Board at Hardy Girls "made me more aware of stereotyping, inequalities" and offered a "better way of addressing them." Practice talking about such issues during GAB meetings helped eighteen-year-old Sam, who is Latina and describes herself as quiet and shy, put her feelings and thoughts into actions and words: "Now

I am able to explain what I do a lot better." Insights she's gained about power and strategy from GAB planning meetings, Cassidy says, have helped her navigate in a world in which "you are not respected unless you have a degree."

"We are equipping girls with the skills not only to talk back and take action but to also talk to their peers about talking back and taking action, and just creating this huge activist movement of teenagers who are mad about what they see and can do something about it," SPARK's Melissa Campbell says. It's a tall order, and there are no shortcuts or easy answers. "Activist work is hard," Williams says, reflecting on the work she and Jackie Dupont do at Hardy Girls:

> It takes time. You can't just create a lesson plan on activism, you have to spend a lot of time doing the consciousness-raising part of it before you can even think to engage girls who haven't done this work before in making change, and it's easy to get impatient when your end goal is activism. So your end goal can't be activism, your end goal has to be a coalition of girls who trust one another and work together, and a by-product of that can be activist work.

This work is an investment—in girls, in their relationships, their quality of life, and, by extension, in our schools and in the society we want. On the ground, in her work with girls of color in the Sisters in Strength program at Girls for Gender Equity, Amina Harris says, the goal is to "understand we're here planting the seeds of consciousness," knowing that the "social justice lens that they develop here will be carried with them into academic and also social spaces, in the form of self-advocacy skills that help them navigate healthcare, employment, housing." Such experiences, SPARKteam member Katy says, "support girls through that process of growing up, figuring out who we are," and offers perspective so they can see beyond the personal, "realizing that these things that impact our lives are not our fault, and helping us deal with them a little bit, and figure out how to articulate it." For Izzy, "it's like really trying to help you become the person you want to be."

The Importance of Calling BS

We can think of feminist activist spaces as systems that open up other systems to scrutiny, always in the service of addressing injustice. In environments that support the development of critical consciousness, girls are encouraged to connect with and interrogate the world they live in, to ask impertinent questions, like "How did this come to be?" "Who says so?" and "Who benefits?" As they become more comfortable and trust builds, we can be certain girls will practice on us, "calling BS," as Montgomery says, on adult assumptions about girlhood, our version of feminism, our unconscious white, middle-class, able-bodied cis privileges. Our commitment is to girls and to the work we are doing together in these moments.

If critical consciousness emerges from relationship and criticality is a practice, then such moments are opportunities for girls to challenge assumptions, name experiences, and unpack barriers to inclusion. As hard as it is to stand in for adultism or to represent the barriers and injustices girls so often confront, I remind my students who facilitate girls' coalition groups for Hardy Girls that these are the moments we've worked so hard for. I remind them that this is not personal; it is bigger than them. These challenges from girls signal commitment to us and to the work. They are signs of curiosity, healthy suspicion, and a refusal to accept the surface explanations for things. The groundwork is in place for deeper conversations about power and privilege. I encourage them to listen, to step in, not away, and to seek out or create activities that allow girls to explore more deeply what they are just beginning to name.[12]

In the end, if we stay present, we can expect and hope girls will learn to identify what media critic Jon Stewart, in his final *Daily Show* soliloquy, called "pernicious, premeditated, institutional BS,

designed to obscure and distract."[13] The kind of BS that makes
"bad things sound like good things" and makes us feel a little
crazy. "The best defense against BS," Stewart argues, "is vigilance."
Critical consciousness, then, is "an I-Spy of BS," that requires an
"if you smell something, say something" call to action. We can't
really do something about a problem, as the women and girl activists profiled in this book underscore, until we can see and call BS.
Thinking critically is about knowing things and feeling things and
it's also about a process of naming and understanding these things
in context, the ways they work and who they benefit or hurt. In
the end, it's about claiming as legitimate our power to redefine, to
reenvision, to act in a new way.

CHAPTER EIGHT

A Witness in Their Defense

Loyalty

Sitting in a television-studio waiting room, eighteen-year-old Emma adjusts the skirt of her strapless baby-blue minidress, takes out her makeup compact, and begins applying black eyeliner and shiny red lip gloss.[1] She and fellow SPARKteam member Carina have been invited to talk on a national morning news show about the campaign they're leading to pressure *Teen Vogue* to no longer digitally alter girls' faces and bodies. The adults who have been collaborating with the girls on the action for the past few months glance with concern at the strip of skin between the hem of Emma's miniskirt and the top of her black thigh-high kneesocks, hoping the camera will not reveal what they fear will be judged a contradiction between Emma's appearance and her message.

It's an uncertain moment. Emma is a veteran activist; she's been with SPARK for three years. She's written sharp critiques of sexualization, publicly protested media sexism, and she's fought for her right to dress as she likes. Emma's clothing choices and makeup the day of her television interview reflect a conscious awareness that her body is a highly visible site for both youth protest and celebration of sexuality. And she understands the dilemma she and SPARK face. "I think the irritating part is that if

I'm in a short skirt, not only am I going to be judged for that, but the institution that I'm working for is going to be judged for that," she says. "I think if you take away that [judgment], rather than my taking away my short skirt or, you know, trying to get me to wear a longer skirt, then that would be more helpful."[2]

The adults' uncertainty has less to do with Emma's decisions—which are, after all, relationally anchored in the feminist work we do together. Working with girls to critically examine the influence and impact of sexualization, harassment, and "choice," we expect such tensions. We know Emma is wide awake and prepared for hard questions. Our concern is about the things none of us can control, like a strategically timed pan of the camera or a sexist comment from the interviewer that could throw her off or a series of cruel online comments following the show.

Effective intergenerational activism requires that we grapple with the contradictions of girls' agency and resistance in a world that demeans and objectifies them.[3] It's not easy to negotiate this reality together, across generations; we worry about girls and we sometimes carry the weight of our own fear that people will judge us by what our younger partners do or say. But doing this work together means living with the starts, stops, and contradictions, listening deeply to girls' voices and experiences, and ultimately trusting girls and supporting their thoughtful and deliberate choices. Knowing Emma's urgent passion to challenge assumptions and disrupt the pressure she feels to change herself, knowing that she is deliberately poking at the tensions, that her choice of clothing and makeup is the equivalent of a public dare, the adults choose to trust her judgment and the preparation work they have done together.

"There are different kinds of fidelity," Jeanette Winterson writes in her coming-of-age novel *Oranges Are Not the Only Fruit*, "but betrayal is betrayal wherever you find it. By betrayal, I mean promising to be on your side, then being on somebody else's."[4] Asking Emma to change her clothes, to wipe off the makeup, knowing what we know about her, about the culture she lives in, about who we are together and what we are trying to accomplish, would be an act of betrayal. Our loyalty is to Emma and the girls we work with, not to our own discomfort or fear or anxiety, not even to our personal version of right and wrong, and certainly not to the oppressive systems the girls struggle within or the people who shore them up.

This loyalty is tested often. When we stand with girls and not with other adults or the way things usually go, our choices are questioned. Anyone who has been a parent recognizes moments like this, when others expect us to speak up, jump in, protect, admonish, smooth away problems, but we don't, because we have negotiated a different trajectory with our child. We have a different agenda, a different understanding of what matters. Our refusal is likely to be read as cluelessness or irresponsibility or bad parenting, maybe even as a weak attempt to be Amy Poehler's "cool mom" from the movie *Mean Girls*. We fear for our child and we worry about the fallout, but we've gauged the risks together and we know that to override her at this moment is a betrayal and that's so much worse. But, man, we can't help thinking that this would be infinitely easier if she, if we, didn't have to take on this judgment or that response.

Both girl activists and the adults who work with them underscore the importance of the kind of trust that's created by passing such loyalty tests. This is where the rubber hits the road, and it requires courage—the courage to give girls power and the courage to stand by them when they use it. If we believe in the consciousness-raising work we are doing together, if we believe in girls' capacity to think critically and their right to come to their own conclusions about what matters to them, and if we really believe risk-taking is good for girls and true leadership involves grappling with possibilities, disagreements, and making the hard choices, then the onus is on us to provide them with all the support we can muster as they make decisions and face consequences.

When Things Fall Apart

I see the struggle to stay on girls' sides most clearly when I conduct workshops for adults who want to enable girls' activism and social-change work. Outside of their families, these are the adults that girls spend most of their time with—staff in girl-serving organizations, social workers, teachers, and guidance counselors. They are enthusiastic about their support for girls' agency. Things run smoothly in these sessions for most of our time together.

Typically I begin workshops by introducing the power of intergenerational partnerships and coalition work. I address the importance of listening to girls, respecting their knowledge, knowing their culture, school, and community. We reflect on what we bring to our work with girls that gets in the way of effective scaffolding—the fears and hopes we've left unexamined, our power and privilege. We consider the systemic barriers to strong intergenerational partnerships. We talk about transparency, strategic support, the courage to stand with girls when things get hard or messy. I share what girl activists have told me about the conditions that enable their best work. I introduce various activist tools, tactics, and resources. So far, so good. Everyone is onboard. Everyone loves the examples of girl-driven activism I share—the culture-jammed ads from *Powered by Girl*, the school-based activism created by Hardy Girls' Girls Coalition Groups, the creative online campaigns initiated by the SPARKteam.

I then arrange participants in small groups and give them a short case-study version of Tierra—the middle-school girl I write about in chapter 2 who names the unfair application of her school's dress code. I ask each group to identify the problem as Tierra sees it, to brainstorm possible actions, choose one, and carry it through using the tools I've given them. This is when things fall apart. Few of the women can get past the problem. Most of the groups embark on heated discussions about media and girls' sexualized clothing, what girls should or shouldn't wear to school, the reasons for enforcing some kind of dress code in schools, what Tierra and the other girls don't yet understand. Someone inevitably argues that girls' bodies are distractions to boys and a debate ensues. Usually someone suggests doing away with the problem altogether by adopting school uniforms. In the end, they cannot get to the task because they cannot accept Tierra's version of events. I'm asking them to create the conditions necessary to support girl-driven activism and they are stuck in what amounts to arguing with a girl about the validity of her experience. Once we arrive at this impasse, and identify it as such, our work together can begin.

Doing this work with girls means letting go of our need to know more or know better and giving up our need to control what girls think and how they feel. We do not have to agree with girls. Our job isn't to persuade them to our point of view. Our job is to help them sort out what really matters to them so they can step into the unknown, act in ways they believe in, risk public dissent. This requires us to remain loyal when other adults insist on girls' ignorance or inexperience. Loyalty means supporting them consistently and publicly regardless of whether we believe what they believe, because what we need to stand behind is their right to figure it out for themselves, to know, and to act.

In their search for what matters to them and their efforts to bring what matters into the world, girls will confront barriers—relational, institutional, cultural. "We are up against the force and weight of something when we attempt to alter the conditions of an existence," Sara Ahmed says. When girls are up against judgments and stereotypes and pressures to be and act in certain ways, loyalty is something we can offer. To again recall the words of Adrienne Rich, we can be a "witness in [their] defense."[5]

Mothers, Sisters, Friends, and Teachers

Loyalty is manifest in different ways, at different times, for different reasons. In her ethnographic study of effective intergenerational projects, educational psychologist Kathrin Walker finds that the most effective adult partners for girls "transcend traditional

reciprocal roles, straddle the adult and youth worlds, and position themselves in a range of ways that allow them to meet the
varied needs of the youth."[6] This maneuverability, this "latitude to
switch roles" [7] when necessary, is only possible if we have proven
to girls that we can be trusted not to abuse our authority and privilege. Such trust, born of different kinds of fidelity, is reflected in
the fluid nature of the relationships between girls and women.
Sixteen-year-old Jasmine thinks of Joanne Smith, founder and executive director of Girls for Gender Equity, sometimes as a "mentor" and sometimes "like a mom," and Smith readily admits, "I
have learned I am the momma of the group." At various times,
girls talk about the women they work with as "muses," "big sisters," "mother hens," "friends," "mentor/support figures," and
even "bosses." "My role shifts a lot," SPARK executive director
Dana Edell explains, "and I think we're all trying to navigate that,
what it means to actually be intergenerational in this way."

It's not an easy thing to navigate, education professor Darla
Linville agrees. "Sometimes I do come down as, you know, 'Listen, guys, that is not realistic.'" She knows that this is a "bubble
burster."

> Sometimes I say to young people, "I think it's too risky, I don't
> think we can do that." Or, "Now's not the time to ask for that."
> I think the hard thing to learn is when to not be the teacher in
> the room. And so one thing that working with young people
> has taught me is that sometimes just being quiet and letting the
> conversation go, letting the young people work out the answer
> instead of giving it is the way to go. I get frustrated with myself
> when I don't, when I fail to make that choice in some situations.
> When I jump in with the answer. If I were to make a big take-
> away lesson, you know, just take time to just be quiet more.

Catching ourselves, choosing to be quiet, listening more—these
are small acts of loyalty. This is the heart of the matter. Relationships can weather all kinds of bubble-bursting moments if we have

a solid relational foundation and cause to trust one another. Girls who feel supported enough to work through the barriers others throw up and who know we have their backs when they engage in public forms of dissent can handle our small acts of mindless adultism. They handle it because they know they can call us on it. Part and parcel of being a girl activist is navigating discrimination at the "overlapping axes of difference and inequality," writes sociologist and activist Hava Rachel Gordon. Girls who push against "institutional, interactional, and individual-level discrimination" are likely to have a frustrating history with adults.[8] For many, intergenerational coalitions are the first time they've experienced adult relationships that don't tip toward condescension or paternalism, and so letting girls practice, offering support as they consider options and struggle with decisions, takes time, energy, and courage. Even so, our support may not be enough. Differences in race, ethnicity, gender and sexual identity, social class, and age persistently raise the specter of possibility that we, regardless of our good intentions, could become another version of the wall, of what girls come up against.

Approaching such differences, confronting barriers and crossing borders, requires what hip-hop feminist activists Ruth Nicole Brown and Chamara Jewel Kwakye describe as "the right combination of humility and skill."[9] We need to admit what we don't know and reflect on what prevents us from listening, relating, and connecting in a deep way.[10] This requires us to stay engaged, curious, and supportive in the face of conflict and disagreement. If we are loyal to the girls we work with, we are open to the possibility that some borders can't be crossed alone. Our willingness to reach out, to collaborate, to take a backseat to those closer to the girls in history, experience, and culture, those who are more familiar and more knowledgeable, speaks volumes to girls about our desire to really know them and support them.

Some of the most powerful and effective youth collaborators are young adults who have grown up in or worked within girl-serving organizations, who have shared girls' histories or experiences. As a former SPARKteam member, and in her early twenties much closer in age to the youth activists she works with, Melissa Campbell has developed close relationships with the girls of SPARK Movement. Her job as program coordinator means connecting with girls daily to ensure actions remain urgent and aren't "lounging to die on the side," she says. "I really try to connect with all the girls on a personal level, and there's this running joke that I'm the big sister/mother hen." It's not an uncomplicated relationship. It also means, she explains, "I'm in this weird liminal space between adult and teen." Dana Edell, SPARK's director, agrees. "Melissa is young enough that she's part of their world mostly; [she deals with] the challenges of being connected with the girls as a friend, but then also needing to step back a little bit as the responsible adult." It's hard at times, but it's a negotiation that enriches the possibilities for the girls. Sharing experiences and working through problems with someone just a little further along on the path—and this includes the skills to lead activist projects—reflects a tried and true educational practice. Campbell sits within what psychologist Lev Vygotsky referred to as the zone of proximal development—that space between what girls can do without support and what they can do with support.[11] Amina Harris, like Campbell just a few years older than the girls she oversees in Girls for Gender Equity's Sisters in Strength program, exemplifies this concept as a relational practice:

> I like to think of myself as one of those really eccentric family members, like an older sister, or a crazy young aunt, because I'm not very much older than them. And I do the silliest things, probably because I have a background in theater, but also because if I'm expecting them to push their growing edge and take risks as a part of our group, it's important for me to model those behaviors and be myself with them as much as I can possibly be.

This ability to embody what it means to be her creative, silly, determined self invites the girls Harris works with to risk their whole

selves in the service of their work together—to be like her, someone who leads from a place of authenticity. It's not easy. But what
she has learned and can teach the girls about transitioning from
novice to "figure of authority" is invaluable. This is, after all, what
we want for girls—to live fully in their power, to authorize their
lives. "It's really important to me that they can see me as all of
those things, and learn, in the process, to take themselves fully into
every new experience and challenge," Harris says. The message she
conveys to the girls is simple but powerful: bring yourself whole
to this work.

> You matter, in the sense that all of you matter. I think that
> sometimes when you take on a position, you know, sometimes
> you might want to compartmentalize, or not be your full self
> in the space, because like, "No, this is where I'll put my orga-
> nizing hat on." But being a community organizer means that
> you're a part of the community, it means that parts of the com-
> munity are reflected in you and you reflect parts of different
> communities.

Like Campbell and Harris, Jackie Dupont began her work with
the Girls Advisory Board at Hardy Girls in her early twenties, just
out of college. Dupont's piercings and dyed hair gave her the cool
factor, and she quickly found that sharing personal experiences as
a kind of older, wiser friend was an effective way to ignite enthusiasm with the high school girls in her charge. Over the years, in
addition to cool older friend, she added adviser, teacher, and muse
to her repertoire.

> I find that my role is often to prompt: "Do you want to throw it
> out to the group for ideas?" "That sounds great, why don't you
> make it known to the rest of the group that you're advocating
> for that at the next meeting." "Let's make sure it's in the agenda,
> bring it up." I'm more of an adviser, I guess, and I am a muse,
> in the language of the work that we do, posing questions and

supporting their best work, and helping them access the things that they need to complete their projects, and also, take an interest in their lives outside of the organization.

Knowing who is required and when—friend, muse, advocate, mother hen, crazy young aunt—isn't possible outside of relationship; that is, without knowing girls well. And knowing girls well is an act of fidelity; it's how we become committed to them, how we become accountable to them.

Persistently on Girls' Side

Being on girls' side looks like small acts of care and encouragement, all the "small conversations that happen on a day-to-day basis," SPARKteam member Alice says, that suggest, "Yeah, you can do that," or in Simone's words, "We're here for you, to support you." It feels like assurance that adults will use their social and cultural capital in the service of the work together; it's faith that when adults say to girls, "What we are doing is changing how things are," Treva says, it's more than "cheerleadery" platitudes. It looks like support that holds when girls take public risks; it feels like certainty that adults and other girls won't crack under the pressure of outside judgments or threats, won't jump ship at proffered enticements of power and resources. As Jasmine explains, "You can feel something all you want, but if you don't have people who back you up, help, speak up . . . it's pointless."

When I ask about loyalty, Jackie Dupont tells me about Natalie and Sarah, two college student "muses" facilitating an eighth-grade Girls Coalition Group, who learned how hard and important it is to support girls in the face of dismissive authorities. The girls in the group wanted to challenge the school-based harassment and bullying they experienced, and so to help them generate ideas Natalie and Sarah shared with the group a variety of activist projects they had found online. The girls were completely taken with the Maine Coalition Against Sexual Assault (MECASA) Backbone

Zone campaign (tagline: "Everyone has a backbone. Use yours."). The campaign includes a series of posters that juxtapose definitions of words with the ways these words are misused to harass: for example, "This is a pansy. / This is a boy who's having a bad day"; "This is a bitch. / This is a girl who speaks her mind."[12]

Dupont recalls Natalie's version of events:

> After the muses showed the posters, the conversation was great. The girls were really excited about educating their peers. They asked [the muses] if they could go get the principal to show her the examples and explain how they planned on using these posters as a model to create their own. When [the principal] walked into the room, the girls started to explain, and they showed her the first one—"This party is so gay. / This party is so boring." As soon as one of the girls read the word *gay*, the principal responded "No!" She explained that in a k–8 school, the posters were not appropriate. She shot them down.

The muses and the girls were stunned and felt they had done something wrong. This feeling prompted Natalie and Sarah to meet with the principal after school. "She was adamant that eighth graders aren't mature enough to handle words such as *gay*, *fag*, and *bitch*, even when they're used in their true definition and not the derogatory phrases that are thrown around quite often in the school," Dupont said. "In the end, the principal thanked the muses for volunteering and that was it."

But Natalie and Sarah knew they couldn't let it go. "[The girls'] energy and enthusiasm for the project was rare and we knew running with their ideas at this time was crucial," Natalie told Dupont. But they were concerned that pushback could get the girls in trouble, could mean the end of the group, might even impact Hardy Girls' relationship with the school. With Dupont's encouragement, they checked in with the school guidance counselor, who, they discovered, was more supportive. And they processed it all with the girls at the next meeting—the principal's reaction, their feelings about the issue, next steps. The girls decided to develop a new action plan. They would document "inappropriate words" for a week. Not only would they count the times they heard such words, but indicate where they heard them and the gender and grade of the speaker. The results were convincing. They heard all the slurs on MECASA's posters, and more. The girls compiled their research and gave it to the guidance counselor, who said she would share it with the principal.

It would be good to know if the principal saw and learned something from the girls' research, but more important was the decision to trust the girls' experiences and choose their passion for this issue over the principal's reaction. In an act of fidelity, Natalie and Sarah brought the problem back to the girls as something to solve together. If the principal's view had been allowed to stand as public reality, what would become of what the girls know to be true from their experiences? They would associate knowing what they know with "the feeling that we did something wrong."

Loyalty in the form of trust and persistent support for girl activists becomes especially valuable in such precarious moments. The principal had a point—in a k–8 grade school the posters, no matter how clever, could be confusing to the youngest students. It would have been easy for Natalie and Sarah to accept the principal's version of the problem as complete and true, and to offer the girls explanations and justifications. Returning to the girls with possibilities instead of platitudes, they turned discomfort and shame into an opportunity to offer a dissenting voice.

Natalie and Sarah gave their small group of eighth graders what other girl activists say they want. It's so important, SPARK-team member Julia says, to have a space where "no one is going to get mad at you . . . or punish you" for things you know, say, or do. It's important to support us, Yas agrees, "even if we decide to do something different" from what the adults want. And the women activists agree. It's essential, Linville says, to create space to process feelings and experiences, to say, "'Wow, this hurts' [and] sit with it all together. Joke about it if need be." In these moments,

SPARKteam member Katy says, "we're learning that even the best activists still learn every day."

Invisible Loyalties

Much of the ways we support girls is invisible to them. The girls in the group were not privy to the conversations Natalie and Sarah had with the principal after school, the guidance counselor, the staff at Hardy Girls—not fully, anyway. They were not aware of the personal and relational work the two muses needed to do, checking in with one another, sorting through their own fears and discomfort, a process that allowed them to return the next week ready to scaffold the girls' new ideas into something tangible.

Psychological research suggests that effective support looks like someone imperceptibly creating the conditions for another's agency.[13] The work Natalie and Sarah did behind the scenes ensured they could return to the group with the information, the questions, the courage to open up possibilities for the girls, to encourage their creative control over the situation. This kind of support is hard to give if we haven't sorted out our own reactions and feelings first. The "invisible" nature of this work does not indicate a lack of transparency, in the ways transparency is vital to effective intergenerational partnerships. There is no reason the muses would not talk with the girls about these meetings or withhold the information they learned. The invisible part is the emotional and psychological work Natalie and Sarah did and how they channeled the results into support for the girls' passion and their agency.

Standing with girls in this sense means spending the time it takes to understand a situation fully and to process and confront our own invisible loyalties[14]—the obligations we feel, the personal debts we owe, the people or systems we fear our actions might betray. If we don't do this work, we risk derailing girls. Our ambivalence, anxiety, even resentment, unnamed and unprocessed, can inadvertently surface as inconsistency and uncertainty. Naming the invisible threads that tie us to expectations, norms, and conventions makes it more likely we will be trustworthy and accountable partners. We are free to recalibrate; we can recognize, Linville says, "the moments where going off course is the necessary direction, to get to where we are going." We can respond flexibly, trusting our ability to see more clearly and respond well to what's in front of us.

Girls, especially younger girls, don't necessarily know how to spot an opportunity to do activist work, says Hardy Girls' Megan Williams. "They may just say 'Yeah, you're right, that really does suck and let's move on.'" So knowing how and when to offer support requires not only "a combination of skill-building and consciousness-raising, but also standing with girls as they begin to take baby steps towards activism." Encouraging an insight, kindling a spark, supporting the earliest inklings of injustice in ways that resonate with girls is a difficult thing. Our adult tendency to feel excitement at the possibilities in front of girls means we can too quickly step in with ideas and advice—and then it's a short leap to taking over.

If we want young girls to engage in feminist activism, we have an obligation to reach out to them and make their transition into the movement both easy and fun. We don't want to become another kind of barrier, another kind of force girls come up against. Yas sought out feminism as an outlet and safe haven in her early teens, but soon discovered a wall of "massive academic terms":

> When I was first coming into feminism, I felt like it was all for adults in a way. Everything was really academic and quite scary and there were loads of books written by these amazing women which I read and I thought were really, really cool. But I thought this is what feminism was all about; all these amazing people that I was never going to reach. Here I was a kid—I felt alienated in my school because I felt like I developed these views that no one else really had. And then I felt alienated in the feminist community because everywhere I was going it was adults discussing

things and I felt like there were really no other young people who were really into this.

Yas needed the adult feminists she met to cultivate a much better understanding of girls' experiences and find ways to build bridges to girls' everyday lives: "A lot of the time when girls first come into feminism," she explains, "it can be a bit disorientating and a bit confusing because it is completely abstract compared to anything we have ever seen before. You know, like, completely different than teen fiction and what we are taught in school, which is all a lot more simplified." The pressure girls feel, Yas says, to "understand everything straight away and if they don't that means that they are really just not onboard" not only "really turns young people off," it can feel like betrayal. Girls like Yas are quick to call out feminists for their hidden loyalties to academic discourse and disciplinary conventions that shut girls out and discourage their participation even while paying lip service to "giving young women a voice."

One of the things grassroots feminist organizations do effectively is make abstract ideas concrete and accessible to younger girls through curricular materials, programs, and training. Organizations like those represented in this book certainly, but many others across the country, reach out in creative ways to young feminists. About-Face ("Don't fall for the media circus") in San Francisco uses media literacy and activism as consciousness-raising tools; SOLHOT (Saving Our Lives Hear Our Truths) in Champaign-Urbana, Illinois, uses hip-hop feminism to "create spaces to affirm Black girl genius"; Project Girl in Madison, Wisconsin ("unmediafy your life"), combines visual art and critique of consumer culture to activate girls; and Ma'yan ("Listen for a change") in New York City offers feminist, social justice, and leadership training through their use of participatory action research. They are the tip of a loyal-to-girls feminist iceberg and they are all accessible online.[15] We don't have to reinvent the wheel.

CHAPTER NINE

"A Politics of Participation"

Supportive Coalitions

As "a shy person" when she joined the SPARKteam at seventeen, Celeste felt like "a fish out of water." During her first summer planning retreat in New York City, "I mostly hung back," she said. The leadership was mostly white and from New York, and as a Mexican American girl from San Diego, she found it "a little bit hard to fit in." That year "I kinda wrote a few blogs," but "overall I wasn't involved that much and I didn't know the people very much." This changed soon after she arrived in New York for the second summer retreat.

During an intergenerational brainstorming session, activist Shelby Knox pointed out that the Doodles on Google's home-page—the clever animated drawings that replace the Google logo on noteworthy days like the birthdays of historical figures—seemed to commemorate the accomplishments of mostly white men. The girls were taken with this observation, and when they split into "action teams," a group of five, including Celeste, chose to strategize and pitch a Google Doodle action plan to the entire team. They would research gender and race disparities, educate the public, and pressure Google to do the right thing, to diversify their

Doodles. A tall order, but they were undaunted. The "Doodle Us" campaign was one of five selected by the girls that year.

Almost immediately after her team began their group discussion about this action, Celeste remembers, "I started getting to know people a lot better." Together the girls embarked on an ambitious research project counting and analyzing the Doodles with respect to race and gender, beginning with Claude Monet, the very first person honored by Google in this way. From 2010 to 2013, they discovered and later blogged, Google celebrated 434 individuals in Doodles on its various homepages throughout the world. An overwhelming 357 of those people were men—and 275 of those men were white. 77 Doodles celebrated women—but only 19 celebrated women of color.[1] The girls wrote a detailed eleven-page report illustrating their findings, complete with bar graphs and pie charts.[2]

Convincing research in hand, and with the support of the full team of girls and adults, Celeste and two of her team members, Katy and Mehar, launched a petition asking Google to "better represent the diversity of the world we live in." They created a short video about their findings, pointing out the impact such a distorted "sign of who matters" makes on everyone, but especially on young girls of color.[3] And to make it very easy for Google to find people to celebrate, the girls created a "This Could Be Google Doodles" Tumblr page, "compiling a list of historical heroes that totally deserve Doodles," such as Audre Lorde, Coretta Scott King, and Dorothea Dix.[4] They sent press releases about their findings and actions to the media, and throughout it all, Celeste, who had risen to a leadership role within her team, blogged:

> This project is bigger than Google Doodles. It's about becoming visible in a society that erases our history and our existence; it's about acknowledging and celebrating our part in building this world. So we're asking Google to Doodle Us: . . . women, people of color, people with disabilities, queer people, trans people.

We're asking Google to draw our histories, our achievements, our strength, our heroes, our fighters and foremothers. You can't keep ignoring us. We're here, and we've always been here.[5]

Working on this action with the other girls and with SPARK's programs coordinator, Melissa Campbell, was a powerful experience for Celeste. Issues that felt "broad and abstract" were suddenly grounded in experience. Relationships deepened. Uncertainties about her place on the team subsided. "We would get together and kind of have a conversation," she says of her time planning the action. "We would brainstorm or talk about the stuff that still needed to get done, and we would all throw out ideas and it definitely felt like my ideas got equal consideration to their ideas." It wasn't an easy road. Sometimes it felt "overwhelming" and sometimes Celeste carried more of the load than the others, but "I think, at the end of the day we were all working . . . getting the action done."

Campbell's role became especially important to Celeste as she took on more responsibility for the action. She relied on the SPARK adults support and her experience offered in alliance, in coalition.

It didn't feel like there was too much of a power structure between us because she was willing to do the same work I was doing. She didn't just check in occasionally and relegate the boring or messy stuff to me—instead, she got right down and did all the messy stuff beside me. She double-checked my work and I double-checked hers. We were in constant communication. I would roll out of bed in the morning and the first thing I would do was return Melissa's emails.

Working in coalition with Campbell meant "when I was struggling with a certain aspect of the project, she was too," that "she was there to guide me and also actually to do the work with me." It meant "she was a really big part of the project," not as an adult in control but as someone with "an equal stake in the project," as someone who "put in a similar amount of work" and so "we were on the same page about its message and significance."

Coalitions thrive for the same reasons they are challenging: they're made up of a diverse collection of people, Celeste says, who "come together to work toward the same goal." Effective coalitions ensure creativity, a wider range of knowledge, skills, and tactics; many hands, strength in numbers, and a broader reach. They also require ongoing discussion and debate, openness and flexibility, a willingness to compromise for the sake of the larger good. This is both wonderful and hard work, Celeste learned, because "activism tends to come from a really, really personal place." Finding other girls and adults whose passion for social justice intersects at that same personal place is powerful, but it's also an ongoing challenge, she says, to be "inclusive of other people who have different identities than we do," because we all "have our own experiences at the forefront."

To work effectively on a common issue, across differences, the girls say, they need to know and feel accountable to one another. For Celeste, a common project led to deepened relationships. For SPARKteam member Izzy, it's a "step-by-step process" that begins with "building relationships, then you start planning and brainstorming, and then you do the actions." Either way, trusting relationships play a vital role in creating and sustaining effective coalitions of girls. Celeste explains:

> A lot of the activism is not just the campaigns we do; it's sort of the fact that all of us are there for each other. All the girls are really, really supportive and I think just creating a space where we can rant to each other and be supportive of each other and comforting when something is going wrong. I think that is a form of activism in itself, and that's really important to me and I'm so grateful to have that.

Megan Williams agrees. In her work with Hardy Girls, she's discovered that "girls want to feel really invested in a group and invested in the relationships they create in the group." For girls who feel isolated or anxious in their schools and communities, what Jessica Taft terms a "politics of participation"[6] is especially powerful. They seek out and embrace activist communities, not only because these communities speak to issues they care about, but because they are reassuring and pleasurable. "When I work with other girl activists, it feels like we're just normal teenagers," SPARKteam member Katy says. "We hang around and talk, and we get really excited about our ideas, and then strategize how to make them work; it's creative and supportive and really fun." Such experiences underscore the importance of what Taft calls "deeply collective" spaces where communication, friendship, and openness flourish.[7]

Supportive relationships and fun experiences can sound so simple and so, well, apolitical. But for many girls who feel like the lone feminist or activist in their school, it's a lifeline, drawing them to collective engagement and meaningful civic work. "We get so many emails from girls that are like, 'I thought I was crazy until I found your website,'" Campbell says, "'I can't believe that there are other girls who feel the same way I do and I can't believe I can do something about it.'" It's true, Executive Director Dana Edell says of the girls who join SPARK: "They want to build a community among other young feminists."

> So many of our girls say all the time how isolated they feel at their school, in their community, in their family. They feel like they're the only feminist—nobody understands them, they get made fun of, they get teased, they get all the stereotyped, ridiculous things, you know, across the board. One of our girls is in tenth grade, this breaks my heart, she started a feminism club at her high school and then a bunch of boys got mad and they started a "macho club." And so the macho club meets across the hall from the feminist club.

For girls worn down by inequities masquerading as neutrality or just the way things are, the possibility of a group of people who see what they see and want to work together on an issue they all care about is exciting. What "motivates the young women to apply for Sisters in Strength," Amina Harris explains, "is really the opportunity to be in a safe space unlike any other space they might have been a part of." This is important, she says, because "it's very rare to have the opportunity to be in a space full of just young women and folks who identify and feel and be with adults who imagine your whole identity and who don't discourage you from being who you are, but also challenge you to be present and hold yourself accountable."

For Celeste, who describes herself as someone with "a lot of social anxiety," this combination of safety and challenge was especially important. "What's really exciting to me about SPARK is that I can do this work in a setting that's still really comfortable for me. I mean, I still get pushed sort of beyond my comfort zone, but not so much that I just kind of want to like give up altogether and run away from it."

Coalition-Homes

In "Coalition Politics: Turning the Century," her classic 1983 address to the West Coast Women's Music Festival, activist-musician Bernice Johnson Reagon distinguishes the safety and comfort of home from the hard, demanding work of coalition building. "Coalition work is not done in your home," she says. "Coalition work has to be done in the streets. And it is some of the most dangerous work you can do. And you shouldn't look for comfort." Home, on the other hand, is where you're fed; it's the place where you are shored up, cared for, and loved so you can "go back and coalesce some more."[8]

The girls, perhaps because they cannot yet invent the homes they want, make no such clear distinction. They carve out homes within their coalitions. Small subgroups come together around interests, crossing boundaries of age, gender identities, race and cultural background, even geographic location. As their actions develop, their relationships deepen; girls meet up with adults to plan in private Facebook chats or on conferencing platforms like Zoom or, if they live close enough, in coffee shops. "We have to have personal relationships with each other, so that we feel comfortable sharing our ideas with each other and then, like, creating main ideas from other smaller ideas we each have," Cassidy explains, referring to her work on the Girls Advisory Board at Hardy Girls. Simone, her fellow GAB member, agrees. "It's sort of a home base. We learn about activism together as a group and so our friendships, I think, help us to be able to be active in society more." Friendship helps the girls bond with "and feel comfortable around each other, and we learn about activism through that, like through each other, we learn about things, what other people have done in their communities." It starts to feel "like we've been close friends all our lives," Alice says of the girls on the SPARKteam. Such coalition-homes are "the way to be heard," Simone explains, opportunities "to talk to other people passionate about the same things . . . to build connections and do things about the things you think need to be changed."

Celeste, Simone, and the other girls refer to their fellow activists, young and old, as "friends" and "allies," but most often, "sisters." Sisterhood might sound a bit old school in some circles—it's certainly not a phrase teen girls hear very often or see enacted in the barrage of "mean girl" media targeting their demographic—but it's not at all unusual to hear girls in any of these coalitions utter a version of sixteen-year-old Amber's advice: "Love your sisters." As Dana Edell says, "I think girls hunger for that kind of sisterhood and solidarity and finding other girls like them. I mean, one thing that they consistently say across the board after the retreat, and even in our online spaces, is that it just feels so good to connect with other girls who feel the same way and who they can talk to about these issues. They're so hungry for that, for those kinds of friendships and relationships." Melissa Campbell agrees: "They need to know that there's someone on the team *with* them. They need to know that even if all these people on the Internet are calling them crazy bitches or whatever that there is a team that has their back, that there is someone working with them."

In this sense, the girls' activist coalitions are their chosen families, where a sense of home makes speaking up and taking risks on the front lines possible. "Everyone gets really passionate and puts their ideas in there," Alice says, which means everyone shares a feeling of vulnerability. Coalition for these girls is a space for "celebrating each other," says Sisters in Strength member Brianna; it's a place to experience the "freeing" feeling of discovering "friends who get it," says Alice. "I trust them a lot; it's not a judgmental space," Jasmine agrees. "We're sisters. We'll work together and support each other."

These coalition-homes can feel a little like beehives, where everyone has a place, a role, and the work gets done in ways that can look chaotic to the uninformed observer—activist planning, coalescing, love, hilarity, recuperation, and support all happening in pockets of activity, all cross-pollinating the work. In this way, the SPARKteam's private Facebook group is both home base and beehive central. On any given day, posts by girls and adults are as likely to be calls for emotional support and personal advice as they are requests for campaign strategy, resources, or organizing information. Coalition happens in the streets, yes, but even there a steady stream of texts and banter tether the girls to their supportive sisters.

Doing Difference

All of this sounds utopian. In reality, it takes continuous effort. It's hard. It's messy. It requires courage. "It's a challenge to be inclusive of people," Celeste admits. It's a challenge to speak up. Sometimes, Julia says, even experienced girl activists can be "hesitant to speak about our problems, especially if we are disagreeing with people." It's tough taking a stand against a collective decision. "It's hard to be a lone voice," Montgomery says, because "not everyone wants to be the person going against everyone."

And there are so many reasons to avoid that "bumpy journey . . . into a discourse of power and difference."⁹ Because the issues that draw girls to activism are so personal, because they seek home in coalition, once they arrive it's easy to lapse into sameness, to collude in silence, to find relief in common ground. It's unlikely girls will have had experiences or know how to "do difference with each other"; how to "'play with' notions of gender, race, and sexuality . . . try on ideas . . . test themselves and each other" without some guidance and support.¹⁰ "You kind of expect that activist spaces are going to be better than the quote unquote 'real world,'" Celeste says. "But, like, it's not always."

Ironically, one of the biggest roadblocks to such work, Celeste discovered, was the fact that "SPARK girls are so friendly with each other and it's such a comfortable environment. Honestly, I love it, but sometimes it's a barrier in the sense that it's more difficult to speak up. Because we know it's going to bring on a moment of discomfort for everyone. And, like, everyone's hesitant to do that." Celeste was completely thrown at her first retreat when, in the midst of SPARK's effort to "foster an environment of fun, friendship, and sisterhood," a teammate made "racist" comments. "One of the things [she] said to me was like, 'Oh, I'm not racist or anything . . . I have Mexican friends, but . . . ' Yeah, the most basic kind of microaggression." New to the team, Celeste wasn't sure she could trust the white women leaders in the room to handle the situation: "The fact that they were totally people that I'd met the day before and the fact that they were white definitely made me like 'I don't know if they'll be supportive or if they're going to just brush me off.'" She had only her past experiences to rely on and those didn't instill confidence. "I wasn't sure about breaking it, interrupting, you know, the friendliness of the group."

Celeste did interrupt. With support from the adults and other girls on the team, she spoke up. But when the girl continued to post microaggressions on the group's Facebook page over the next few months, Celeste asked adults to step in and "just put an end to that right away." Executive Director Dana Edell spoke with the girl and eventually asked her to leave the team. The adults then arranged workshops on power and privilege for the next retreat.[11] These were helpful, Celeste said, but it would have been so much better if it never came to this—if the adults anticipated problems and did preemptive diversity work, like "more specific conversation about how racism and classism and stuff like that play out within the group."

> I feel like if we had some kind of training on microaggressions and the way racist and classist remarks, like, play out; if we had that conversation during the [first] retreat, this girl wouldn't have said this to me because she would have realized, like, you know, that's one of the most common things people say, and then they go on to do something racist. Like girls will start recognizing like, "Oh, I've kind of said that, so maybe I should reconsider what I want to tell this person." And also it can be really validating for the people who have gone through those experiences to hear that it happens all the time and it's like not OK. And so that way they'll be able to put a name on whatever they experience, and they'll be more comfortable speaking up about it.

Everyone learned valuable lessons. Adults learned how we can inadvertently enable a collective impulse to lean toward sameness. We all learned how the comfort and friendliness of sisterhood can be misinterpreted by some as permission to say anything and put pressure on others to "let things slide." We learned how important it is to prepare girls to work effectively across difference and how "it's not working," as Celeste says, when "the education of [some] girls is coming at the expense of the other girls." And so the next group of new SPARKteam members entered with the training Celeste wished she'd had from the start. All of us, even girls fully committed to activism, to feminism, and to coalition work,

Celeste says, have "the potential to perpetuate social norms and power dynamics or oppression."

> We're all products of this society. It's entirely possible that I am going to perpetuate homophobia or sexism or transmisogyny or something like that because I'm very privileged in those areas, so it's entirely possible that I have the potential to perpetuate that oppression. And kind of the same thing goes, like sometimes we think, "Oh a thirteen-year-old girl, like what do they know about racism? They can't be racist yet because they are so young." But it's entirely possible that they can be.

The lessons we learned are especially important for an organization like SPARK, Celeste says, an organization with mostly white adult leaders working in coalition with girls of color. "Sometimes adults don't realize the weight that their words hold with younger girls of color, since white authority figures can be super intimidating. . . . Often girls tend to think they're the ones in the wrong."

> I mean, a fourteen-year-old is going to have a different perspective on adult fallibility than a twenty-one-year-old. It's hard for anyone to call out a figure of authority, particularly regarding stuff like race. But younger girls especially are used to just ignoring their own discomfort and listening to what adults say. Because their relationship with adults in school and at home is largely about respect and not challenging authority, they're so much less likely to speak up if something feels wrong, if they even realize it's the adults' actions that make them uncomfortable.

Celeste's insight was enormously valuable as the adults in SPARK sought to understand the nuances of power in relationships across age and race. If we as adults hope to work in coalition with girls, to create the conditions for girls to become full contributing partners in our movement, we have to be vigilant, reflective, and commit, as Ruth Nicole Brown says, to do the kind of hard, honest work it takes to "deconstruct the mythology of the border."[12]

White adults working with girls of color need to consider how we inadvertently enable a collective impulse to lean toward sameness and do our best to prepare girls to work effectively across difference. It takes time, and energy, and careful attention to what girls are saying to provide what Katy describes as "a safe space, where girls feel open to talking about their ideas, and where girls feel like the issues that impact their lives matter." Since power structures related to difference exist so deeply in nearly all other parts of our lives, it is naive to assume we can dismantle them easily. But we have to persist in the hope that we can create the conditions for girls and women to work in coalition and come to critical consciousness together. Girls need, as Celeste says, "adults who can relate." They need adults who listen to them, have faith in them, but they also need adults who really get them. This means, quite simply, that girls of color need women of color involved in their intergenerational coalition work.

Building Coalition

No matter how much you believe in girls, Celeste tells adults, "Don't expect girls to solve problems you're uncomfortable with or know little about. Take responsibility for learning." This means a willingness to step in and step up, even if, in the moment, we're not quite sure what to do. As Girls for Gender Equity's Joanne Smith explains,

> So many times it's managing your own emotional intelligence and also being able to watch group dynamics and see what's happening. Many times well-intentioned advocates don't know when to step into a group dynamic that may be exploiting a young person, or may be hurtful or go too far. . . . Even if they know it's wrong. But even when we don't know what the right answer is, [it's important] to say, "Wait a minute, that doesn't

sound or sit right with me, let's check in," and to interrupt a process that allows for us to learn together as well as models active engagement with what is happening in the group process.

This is what effective, accountable intergeneration coalition looks like. As we expect girls to risk, we have a special obligation to listen, to remain open and vulnerable, to learn and grow, and to be honest with them. "It's very easy to see sixteen-year-old girls of color who are brilliant, who have an analysis on social justice issues, and who show up happy many times and be in awe of them, like 'Wow they're just amazing, I was not this brilliant at sixteen!'" Smith says, "but then let things they say that clearly demonstrate internalized sexism, racism, homophobia, et cetera, and that are just wrong or hurtful to each other, slide because it makes you uncomfortable to address it." In those moments we have to step in, she says. It's "a disservice to allow those things to slide."

> Interrupt them. If they're not showing up with passion for each other or with the social justice consciousness that we're representing and it's harmful, then it's our job to step up as advocates, to speak to them about it, name the misstep—not to embarrass them, not to shame them, but to have that teaching moment. I teach interns this in their first year, especially if they're not used to working with conscious black girls. If they can't address what is clearly inappropriate language or behavior because they feel uncomfortable then, again, they're doing our youth a disservice. They should question their biases and expectations they have of black youth and they must stretch in their own growth and learning. This is the sweet spot where young people can see that we authentically value them and hold them in high regard.

This can be a precarious balance for adults, especially when girls and adults take pride in fostering an intergenerational partnership where "girls have the power to settle conflicts and disagreements," Girls Advisory Board member Lily says. But even then, perhaps especially then, girls say they want adults who will be there when things threaten to fall apart to support them when they risk interruption and disagreement and to challenge them to be their best selves.

Creating coalition is creating the conditions necessary for girls to experience both "OMG, that's how I can change this!" and "I don't have to do this alone," Edell says. Successful intergenerational activist projects provide generous opportunities for relationship building that include pondering what it means to work together across differences. By offering a rich and fun combination of training, cookouts, workshops, dances, and action planning, girls and women together develop connections that deeply impact and strengthen their work. Learning to trust one another ensures girls feel secure enough to "face criticism," Julia says, and risk public dissent. Such confidence emerges in relationship, the result of receiving others' trust and respect, experiencing the power to move through disagreement and to affect others. Coalition, the girls tell us, is the groundwork, the foundation of their courage. Once girls know they are not alone, once they feel connected, understood, and supported, the rest is flexing their new activist muscles.

CHAPTER TEN

Trust and Transparency

The Possibility of Intergenerational Partnerships

Adult partnerships with youth are rare and wonderful things. They're like "pockets of oxygen"[1] where everyone can breathe and feel the expansive possibilities of working together. But, as the girls say, that good feeling doesn't happen very often. Mostly adults structure or determine the course of events without girls' input. Mostly girls experience well-intentioned forms of adultism. "It's so annoying, in any sense, to have adults look down on you because you are young," says SPARKteam member Izzy, or, as Sisters in Strength youth organizer Cheyanne says, to "talk down to us" and say things like "I know more about this than you do." But that's the way it usually goes.

Girls tend to be more politically conscious and committed to activism than boys, and yet adult constraints and protections can make it harder for girls to engage in public forms of dissent.[2] Parents, for example, worry more about the consequences for their daughters, keep closer track of their whereabouts, and expect less independence from them. Girl activists report that they do not feel sufficiently supported by adults, who tend to see them as cute, incapable, and in need of adult guidance.[3] In addition, popular media messages about girls' empowerment in the form of appearance, sexual commodification, and purchasing power create barriers to their activism and invite girls to desire and embody the very conditions that serve to constrain, restrict, and subordinate them.[4] It's not surprising, then, that girls so love working with women who invite them in as respected and capable political actors with good ideas.

The girl activists I spoke with gravitate toward women who "listen to you talk," Izzy says, and who realize that "you know more than [other] people say you know." Such women take them seriously and want to learn from girls. Their first assumption is that girls are capable; their impulse, Treva says, is to give girls "free reign and see how things go." They "don't shut people down, just saying 'no' or 'that's a stupid idea,'" Montgomery explains. And by simply saying yes for a change, "they're making a difference in a world where so many things are decided for us." This sense of possibility is inviting. "I think it's super cool that I get to educate some adults," Izzy says. "That's a really good feeling." Celeste loves the "casual" horizontal nature of the intergenerational activist work she's done with SPARK. "It's kind of like, it feels sometimes like we're colleagues or coworkers."

Adults who treat girls as equals, with full power to generate ideas and impact decisions, Cassidy says, "know our voices are just as important." Girls may not come into partnerships with the same level of knowledge or experience, but they bring what's unique to them and their situations. As their voices are valued, they own their power and they begin to see how important and necessary they are to the success of the work together. "Without young people, there would be no Sisters in Strength," Brianna acknowledges proudly—no place quite like that program where girls of color come together to define community problems and bring their knowledge and passion to creating girl-driven solutions.

When Izzy says she "loves it" when women "treat me as an adult," she's not saying she believes she is the same as an adult or that she always knows as much or has as much expertise. She's saying that she loves being a worthy partner, which is so different from her usual experience of working with adults who "talk down to me like I'm small, below them." She loves relationships in which she is valued as herself. She especially loves working with adults "who will treat you like a human being and will have conversations with you and will let you swear and will let you communicate like you want to." That is, adults who don't police her passion and her rage; adults who make space for all of her.

The women activists understand this. "So many people do the work on behalf of young people," Joanne Smith says. "[At Girls for Gender Equity] we like to say that we do the work 'with' and 'stand with' young people, because it's necessary for all of us to show up one hundred percent when doing this work." Melissa Campbell knows the SPARK girls she works with bring something essential and unique to the partnership. "Girls' voices need to be at the center," she says. "It's really important that girls are at the forefront of this because they're the ones who know what it's like living in this world as girls and young women."

Such partnerships are grounded in respect for what each brings to the work. Adults "know so much . . . and kids know so much," Izzy says. "Listening is a two-way street: I'll listen to your ideas if you listen to mine." Sixteen-year-old Yas of *Powered by Girl* agrees. "Everybody obviously has their opinions, and it's about everyone sharing them collectively." Intergenerational partnerships really work, says SPARKteam member Katy, "when everyone in the group feels like they have a stake in the conversation and what the group is doing. Their ideas are not only heard but are actually acknowledged, and if members of the group are of different ages, the age gap doesn't act as a barrier, but instead really helps foster mutual respect." In the ideal world, such partnerships are spaces "of intergenerational dialogue, where the voices of kids and adults are each valued for their different contributions."[5] In reality, without organizational checks, consistent practices, and a conscious effort to ensure inclusion and fairness, they risk falling back into the habitual recentering of adult power.

It's not always easy for girls to trust adults with what they know or to speak up when their contributions are disrespected.

"It takes a lot of guts [for girls] to say to adults 'I call shenanigans, this is BS,'" explains Montgomery. There are risks involved. Girls bring histories of adult disrespect, mistreatment, and betrayal with them. So the onus is on adults, SPARK Executive Director Dana Edell says, "to do a good job of being incredibly open from the beginning so girls know that we're going to be honest with them." Creating partnership is intentional work, requiring thoughtful observation, a willingness to track and attend to the relational impact of potential barriers—not simply because of age, but also because of culture, race, class, gender identity, ability—all those things that make a difference in how we experience power and privilege and thus influence our ability to communicate and trust one another. It means inviting girls to think together with us about the *possibility* of partnering and then remaining open to adjustment and critique of the process. As Edell explains, "We are constantly asking the girls for feedback and engagement to talk about the way they feel they are interacting with us."

"Working in partnership with children requires that adults leave aside the role that society has often prescribed to them of being the teacher with all the answers," children's rights advocates Natasha Blanchet-Cohen and Brian Rainbow argue. "We are partners seeking answers to creating a better world."[6] All of the women activists talk about building in time and opportunity to reflect on what it means to work together and what partnership looks like in different circumstances. All ensure shared input and ownership of the work. In SPARK Movement adults and girls work together, for example, to address the knowledge and diversity gaps in the team and together review nominations for new members each year with this in mind. "I'm calling every member and asking who and what they think is missing from the team; what girls, voices, how can we make the group more diverse," Edell explains. When the nominations are in, a committee of girls and adults consider that input and advice as they review applications together. For SPARKteam member Maya, this is an example of intergenerational partnership: "We worked together in pairs. I liked that Melissa and Dana [the adults] did one section together, and it wasn't like I was with Dana and I was waiting for her vote to come in before I decided what I thought. I was reviewing my section with another girl, like reading through, and if Celeste and I said a girl wasn't going to be good for the SPARKteam, they never read that application. Like, they trusted us on that."

Figuring It Out

Adult activists bring experience and organizational skills to their partnerships with girls. As good partners, they offer this expertise in ways that open girls up to the big picture, help them find their own rhythm without becoming lost in the possibilities. "I think the challenge for [girls] is not feeling overwhelmed by this, like 'Oh my gosh, we have to come up with the project and it has to like make sense,'" says Amina Harris, reflecting on her work with Sisters in Strength. "Sometimes it's just trusting the process, trusting that they will have a finished product, that they will want to share with people and want to celebrate."

Our work as adults is to create the conditions for girls to become full contributing partners, to develop and take ownership of the work. This is a true challenge, because there is resistance all around—not just from other adults, but from girls too. Girls are required to accommodate to adult-made systems simply because it's easier and quicker for adults. Adults are used to taking power in these moments. Girls are used to giving power away if they don't want to cause a ruckus. Breaking this cycle requires vigilance and will. It takes lots of practice to consistently provide what Katy describes as "a safe space, where girls feel open to talking about their ideas, and where girls feel like the issues that impact their lives matter." In Julia's words, it takes an adult committed to letting girls "figure it out"; someone who asks the kinds of questions that reveal what girls know about the world around them and creates the kind of space that enables girls to share that knowledge. This is not a one-off. It's an ongoing process of discovery and rediscovery for both girls and adults. It requires, Darla Linville says, reflecting on her action project with queer youth, "a lot of time talking about power and talking about what we wanted to get out of it," and being "open to negotiation and ongoing conversation in the group in terms of saying, 'Yes this is a good idea,' 'Yes this is the right direction,' or 'No this isn't going to work,' 'We need to rethink this,' 'This doesn't make sense.'"

Beyond the hard first step—simply getting to the place where we can imagine girls as partners—intergenerational collaborations require uncovering and revisiting adult labor that's typically invisible to girls. Like roadies at a concert, our efforts can be taken for granted. We can run to the store for supplies or tweak petition language. We can make things happen or make things go away with the right call. We can smooth out tensions and take shortcuts. This is what it means to have power, and it is seductive for everyone. But every time we do these things without sharing and talking about them, without agreeing on them together, we subvert our partnership. We take a step toward making this about us—our timing, our egos—and we brush the edges of manipulating situations and tokenizing the girls we're working with. Effacing our work or our access to information and resources might make things easier—we can just get it done—but it's not partnership. We experience partnership when we discuss our options, when we talk about possibilities together, when we share decisions, when we inventory our resources, even when, or especially when, we compromise for the sake of the greater good.

As Treva says, everyone knows that "people listen to adults." Sam, eighteen, agrees. "People don't take you seriously as a girl. It's sad, but true." As partners, girls and adults consider together how to address this reality; how best to use that precious adult privilege strategically. For this reason, intergenerational partnerships can sometimes look adult-led when, in fact, girls and adults are partnering well, making key decisions behind the scenes and doing the majority of the planning together. As adult partners, we can use our power to offer assurances to concerned parents and use our connections to run interference with school officials. We can head off barriers thrown up by other well-intentioned adults. Sometimes this means enlisting the help of others or setting up meetings. And sometimes it's speaking truth to power or absorbing the risk when an action shakes up the status quo.

This agreed upon behind-the-scenes partnership increases the likelihood that actions will succeed. In a study of youth-led activist organizations, sociologist Rachel Hava Gordon discovered that success over time depended on youth working with adults who were willing to use their power strategically for youth causes. For this to be possible, adults and youth together need to reflect on adult tendencies to take over.[7] Such trusted adult partners can provide a "legitimizing 'face'" for the group when necessary by "strategically work[ing] around other adults to facilitate student organizing," and "offer[ing] a passport into adult-dominated spaces such as schools, retreat centers, and even social justice networks."[8] But this can backfire without ongoing communication and agreement.

The key to all of this is trust, and fundamental to trust is transparency. The girls say they are fine with adult support and even some amount of adult control at strategic moments, as long as everyone knows what's going on, why, and how it serves the larger goals of their work together. When the Girls Advisory Board at Hardy Girls offers their annual Girls Rock! conferences, Cassidy, eighteen, says, "it makes sense for us to develop the presentations and run the workshops and balance it with the adults running the rest." The girls work for months together and with Hardy Girls programming staff and interns to organize the events. When everyone is working well together, girls and adults coordinate like steps in a dance.

Such was the case with an ambitious two-year activist campaign designed by the high school youth organizers at Sisters in Strength.[9] The project began with nine young women of color, many of whom had no prior activist or youth-organizing experience, sitting together in a small office with Girls for Gender Equity staff talking about the realities of sexual harassment. The more the young women shared their experiences of being touched without permission, propositioned in school hallways, and called names, the more they wanted to do something about it.

With training and tools offered by GGE staff, the youth organizers began a lengthy process of gathering information and examples from other students, discussing root causes such as sexism and media, reading existing research, and looking at school and state sexual harassment policies. They learned how to do their own research, developed a data-gathering plan, collected and analyzed over a thousand surveys from girls and boys in middle and high schools in New York City. They presented their findings at the GGE's annual neighborhood Gender Equality Festival and there began to build a wider coalition of youth, adults, and organizations called the Coalition for Gender Equity in Schools (CGES). Amina Harris was one of the youth organizers with Sisters in Strength at the time and describes her role in the development of what became a primary CGES action: to ensure every New York City public school had a federally mandated Title IX coordinator.

> So we were looking at a lot of stuff, and I'm hearing that you were supposed to report harassment to a Title IX coordinator, and I wondered how many people know who their Title IX coordinator is. And so from there, [we thought] let's ask people. So we made phone calls to about two hundred schools. The New York Public School System has seventeen hundred schools, so it was a high enough number to be a valid little survey. And about ten schools actually knew what we were talking about, which is saying a lot.

Harris's question revealed a widespread problem and initiated a full intergenerational effort, not just to collect the data but to plan a series of next steps that connected the youth organizers with key constituencies.

> Adults from the Center for Antiviolence Education and the MANY (Mothers Agenda New York) were helping to do phone

calls and develop this campaign with our young women. Once we got the results and analyzed the results of the survey, the young women and an adult representative of Girls for Gender Equity met with the Office of Safety and Youth Development of the Department of Education. We partnered with the New York Civil Liberties Union to draft a letter to the schools that we could not find information about Title IX enforcement through these phone calls.

In the end, Harris and her fellow Sisters in Strength interns were invited to testify at a New York City Department of Education hearing about their findings and to present a series of "really strong recommendations."

This intergenerational model underpins the organization's approach, Harris explains. "A lot of the campaigns or the projects are really born out of Sisters in Strength ideas and supported by the adults from different organizations and from the adults at Girls for Gender Equity, [who provide] materials and the tools and the means and access to theory." As with Hardy Girls, young women and adults see their roles in activist campaigns as different but coordinated. Their partnerships develop over time as each clearly identifies what they bring and as they discuss openly how best to support the work.

Hard Conversations

Such work together is powerful and often exciting and fun, but it isn't especially easy or natural. There are external forces that impinge and threaten. Adults working with girl activists can have positions within their organizations that make them accountable to external others, like funders, supervisors, and boards. A true partnership means letting the girls know this and how it affects the work we do together. If there's tension between the Sisters in Strength interns and the Girls for Gender Equity staff, it's not about the desire to fully develop a girl-initiated activist project, "it's really about capacity," Harris explains. "We have two full-time staff who are here to drive the campaign and make sure that it has to do with the young women, maybe like forty-six hours on a good week or less, so it's really important we are realistic about what they can do."

It's a similar reality for SPARK and for Hardy Girls—organizations that fund the girls' activist projects. Over the years, SPARK has become more and more open about the structure of the organization, the funding constraints, and the hard decisions adults responsible for the health of the organization have to make. "When we let girls see what it takes to run SPARK, they were blown away," Dana Edell says.

> We do monthly trainings online and the second one was on fund-raising. And during the webinar, I put up SPARK's budget. I was like, "Let's talk. I want you guys to see how much it costs for us to do what we do, who's giving us money, how much money different foundations are giving." And they were really blown away by that. I wanted them to be able to ask questions about it, I wanted them to understand that this is what it takes to do this work. It was really funny, before I posted the budget, I said "How much do you think it costs to run SPARK?" And they were in the range from a million dollars to $20,000, because no one ever asks them to think about any of these things. And I think that's a real disservice to girls, that assumption of mistrust and the assumption they won't understand; that all you have to do is show up. And we don't want the "all you have to do is show up" model at all. They need to really know all of these things that go into the work before you show up.

Honest, transparent intergenerational work means bringing girls into new and hard conversations and negotiating strategic decisions together, "giving us a reason and helping us figure out why something wouldn't work," Simone says, not "deciding for us, [but] to feel like we're in tune about why." Ultimately, as Celeste says, if partnership is going to work it's important that adults not "step in and shut the doors and have conversations behind closed doors."

Adults can feel they're giving up a lot when they commit to intergenerational partnerships. It's true that this work requires relinquishing control, and the benefits—the creativity, new knowledge, shared labor, increased expertise and impact, even the fun—isn't always apparent at first. Sharing power with youth is not something most adults have done before, so this way of working is also time-intensive. It's a cultivated skill, and so we can all expect to botch it now and again. The hardest part of the work is the least predictable, the most uncertain: discussing and negotiating the barriers to effective communication; asking hard questions and listening, being open to persuasion, admitting mistakes, addressing disagreements. It's a radical shift in the ways most of us work with youth, which is why so few adults attempt this work. But as SPARK's Melissa Campbell explains, in spite of what takes place in too many school classrooms and youth-serving organizations, girls are not "just receptacles that you can put information in and get the response and the result that you want."

The key to a good intergenerational partnership, the girls say, is *really* inviting them in. "If [adults] are not willing to hear something, then how can we do what we are trying to do?" Lily wonders. Her worst experiences as an activist, Yas says, were the times when "I felt like it was all for adults." Which, sadly, is the norm. The other girls share a litany of similar experiences, times when adults who said they wanted to work collaboratively treated them, as Cassidy says, "like babies or they [didn't] understand what we were talking about"; times when they were excluded, their decisions overturned; when they were "shut down," Montgomery says, or demeaned with comments like, "Well it really isn't that bad, you are making a bigger deal than it is." Partnering with girls means breaking out of these old patterns. "It's the simplest but it's actually huge and we all do it all the time," Edell says, thinking about her work with the girls at SPARK. "Are we really hearing them or are we just hearing what we want?" Is this for real or an "idealized view of what the partnership might look like?"

The true test of effective partnership is the way adults and girls handle differences and disagreements together. "We try to find common ground and compromise as best as possible," Amina Harris says of her work with Sisters in Strength. But this isn't always easy. What matters is that there is no assumption that adults, simply by virtue of status or age, determine the outcome. "Sometimes girls write blogs that I don't totally agree with and I have to just let that go and trust that this is valuable," Edell says, even when "there are things about this perspective that make me uncomfortable." When disagreements happen between youth and adults, Darla Linville says, "we meet as peers, as equals and decide and agree to work with one another to reach both of our goals. And sometimes those goals might be in conflict and then there has to be a good faith interest on both sides to resolve that conflict, you know, in a way that is respectful of both sides."

Campbell talks about how this good faith effort works with SPARK. "There are times where an organization or someone will approach us and say, 'Do you want to take action on this issue?' and then the adult leadership will take it to the girls and if they're into it, it will happen, and if they're not, it won't," she explains. "It's not like these are our teenage minions, that we can make do whatever we want." In those rare moments when resolving disagreements comes down to practical issues, like funding, or to adult experience, transparency is necessary. For example, when the SPARKteam petitioned *Teen Vogue* to include greater racial diversity in its pages and less photoshopping, adults made the final decision to end the campaign. The magazine had issued a clear rejection of their demands, the media stopped covering the story, and SPARK had other girl-driven actions in the works that needed attention and funding, and so, Edell says, "the adults realized 'this is actually done.'" But the girls didn't agree and so a series of conversations followed. "I think it was hard for some of the girls," Edell says. "They were like, 'Well can't we just do more?'" SPARKteam member Alice remembers this disagreement and what she learned from the process:

> I was really into it and I remember [the adults saying], like, "You know what? [Let's] put this one out to pasture." And I was like, "Wait. What?" I wasn't used to the idea of saying, "Hey, maybe this is just not worth putting our energy into, because these people are like, not really going to care about us." And it was an interesting lesson for me, I think, to hear that. It's like, you know what, maybe this is just not going to work and like not everything is going to work. And having that attitude is really helpful.

Other times the final decision lands with the girls. Alice recalls another disagreement with adults, one she highlights as an example of "taking girls seriously and not pressuring them" to agree. Edell and Campbell presented the girls with an opportunity to support a new documentary film. They could interview the filmmakers and create a study guide of activities and discussion questions to accompany the film. But after previewing the documentary, Alice explains, the girls pushed back.

> The horror story was that [a teenage girl] started buying short dresses and wearing heels and we were all like, "Wait." We kind of had this conversation where we all kind of turned to each other and we're like, "Wait, I don't really like this." And we're like, "Yeah, good, because I didn't like it either." And [the adults] were like, "But this would be a good opportunity to collaborate with them. Look at it this way. Think about these opportunities." We just disagreed. We had this instinct, like, "Well, we think this is like kind of a vanity project for the family and it's also like this alarmist thing of, like, "Teen girls are just going to hell, and they're all the worst and, you know, once you wear a short dress you're, like, just a parent's nightmare." And we were all just like not into it. And, I mean, in the end Dana was like, "OK, I can see

this, and if the girls aren't onboard it's not going to happen." So, you know, they listened to us and I think, took it seriously.

In a partnership, everyone gets to present their best case and decisions lean toward the most compelling argument. Sometimes the adults aren't sure how an action is related to the mission, Campbell explains. "But the girls weigh in and the girls explain, 'This is why, this is how, this is the messaging we'll need to connect with that cause,' and so we go forward." Working with girls ensures actions designed to speak to girls are relevant and meaningful to them, which means adults are reminded just how much the world has changed. Campbell describes such an experience, when SPARK was invited "to sign on to a campaign asking [the novelty store] Spencer's to stop selling sex toys because teenagers shop there."

> Some of the adults were like, "Yeah, this would be a good coalition/partnership," and we asked the girls, and the girls were pretty much overwhelmingly like, "Dude, no way! There are a lot of reasons to hate Spencer's but that's really not one of them. Like why would I not want a teen girl to have a sex toy?" And we were like, "Oh. You're totally right. This is not on point for us, this is not what we're about at all," and so we just didn't sign on. We found another way to get involved, centered around Spencer's awful graphic T-shirts.

Remaining partners in the midst of different assumptions and open disagreement is possible when girls and women have developed an understanding of coalition, when adults take girls' knowledge and experience seriously, and when together they have developed a level of trust that carries them through the hard spots. It's not always pretty and it's rarely easy—people get angry, feelings get hurt, and slights are taken personally, and even if none of that happens, actions fail. But intergenerational partnerships are worth it. They are sites of possibility fed by compassion, generosity, playfulness, improvisation, and humor. Working with girl activists as partners means things break open in the most wonderful and surprising ways. We have the incredible opportunity to work with and learn from experts on what matters now and to use the bit of history and knowledge we have accumulated over the years to influence the present moment, to engage with girls in radical and political work.

CHAPTER ELEVEN

Scaffolding Girls' Activism

Meeting Girls Where They Are

As cochairs of the Girls Advisory Board at Hardy Girls and found-
ers of their high school Gay-Straight-Trans Alliance (GSTA), Treva
and Maya had worked with enough adults over the years to know
what good and not-so-good support looks like. During three years
with their GSTA, for example, the girls endured a dizzying stream
of teacher advisers. There was the one who came to the first meeting with a copy of *Teaching Tolerance* tucked under her arm and
a set of preplanned activities fit for a group of elementary-school
students. The one who seemed totally great until students protested homophobic comments on an online high school memes
site and he resigned in panic, afraid he might be held accountable
if things got out of hand. The one who waltzed in, took attendance,
and announced without warning a series of new rules for the way
the group would operate. And the one who sat quietly in the back
of the room, grading papers.

After this roller-coaster set of experiences, Maya and Treva
drew from what they learned at Hardy Girls to compose a how-to
tip sheet called "Three Essentials for Effective Youth/Adult Partnerships."[1] Defining these essentials—trust, respect, and encouragement—they stress how many of the most common forms of

adultism are the easiest to address. Just extend to girls the same kind of consideration and thoughtfulness adults offer other adults, like consideration for schedules, transportation, a willingness to provide needed information and offer explanations, assurances, and apologies. "All of these are ways to show us that you believe in us and see us as successful partners," they write.

Adult activists offer many kinds of support to girls they work with. Sometimes it's temporary scaffolding in the form of sharing information or skills—how to create a strategy chart, for example, or "power map" their school, or develop a survey to gather needed information. Other times it's material support, like providing transportation and funding for projects. And then there's encouragement and emotional support when things don't go as planned. Whatever form it takes, working with girls requires us to listen well, to be thoughtful, aware of our privilege, and always vigilant about the ways our support can slowly transmogrify into control.

Good support is responsive and consistent. "Our job, as partners in this work," Girls for Gender Equity's Joanne Smith says, "is to help shape and create the conditions for [young women] to have a voice and a platform." These conditions are material, educational, and relational, and they are in the service of enabling girls to take on the issues they feel most passionate about. "I really like the scaffolding metaphor," SPARK's Melissa Campbell says, "because it's a support, without being an overbearing support. It's flexible, it's a little bit shaky, it's not made of brick, you can move it around, it may take different forms—that really well describes what we do."

At Hardy Girls, the Girls Advisory Board relies on such flexible support as they plan their annual Girls Rock! conferences for fourth through eighth graders in central and southern Maine. The girls create all of the content. Working in pairs, they develop short presentations like "Feminism 101" and "Girl Activists Around the World" to present in an opening session, and design workshops they will offer throughout the day to the nearly four hundred girls who attend the two events. As they work, the adults offer scaffold-ing—connections to resources, funding for materials, logistic sup-port, and space to meet and practice. The girls know a lot about how the planning will go because the older and more experienced members of the group pass down knowledge and stories from year to year, but still they rely on staff member Jackie Dupont for ongo-ing advice and feedback.

Anticipating the girls' educational and training needs is high on Dupont's list of to-dos. She schedules monthly meetings and check-ins, relays information, and connects the girls to tools and resources they need to develop their presentations and workshops, offering "any information I have that's relevant, like 'check out this website, check out this article.'" While the girls focus on their research and workshops, Dupont has her eye on the big picture. As the first fall planning sessions begin, a full five months before the conference, she asks the girls what skills they think they'll need in order to do their work well. "Girls make decisions about what we need," Izzy explains. If the girls want a session on public speaking or community organizing, Dupont brings in a workshop leader; if they feel a need for additional media literacy or activism training, she sets it up. "We know how to run this conference and we know how to execute it," Izzy says, but Dupont is there to ensure that the girls, especially the new members of the group, get what they need and develop skills. She reminds them to consider their audience, the age of the girls they are reaching, and to build in time and space to practice their presentations beforehand. "It's not very easy to fail," Simone explains, "because people [both the older girls and adults] are advising us and making sure every step of the way ev-erything is working."

As the conference approaches and the girls fine-tune their workshops and presentations, adults at Hardy Girls, Cassidy says, "contribute by setting things up, making calls, making sure schools can get girls there, scheduling rooms." After the conference, Du-pont says, she and the girls meet together and do a "plus/delta," a simple evaluation exercise, and she asks the group to reflect: "What are some things that you wished you knew but didn't? What do you want to learn more about or get better at?" The hope is that they will then "take that information and identify people who could lead new skill-building trainings for next year."

Scaffolding girls' activism in this way, Hardy Girls president Megan Williams explains, "is very hands-on." But it's less around directing girls and "more about identifying what kind of supports they need and how we can supplement." And it's typically very fun. Combining the energy and fresh ideas the girls bring to their activism with the knowledge and support from adults, Izzy says, leads to "workshops, dance parties, and trainings that combine fun and education."

SPARK offers a similar kind of scaffolding, even though support is primarily online. "Communication is key," Executive Director Dana Edell says. "Supporting them in private Facebook groups, having conference calls when they're planning an action, arranging monthly check-ins [on platforms like Zoom or Google Hangout]." Providing this kind of infrastructure allows the girls to focus on their work, to determine next steps. There's a kind of intergenerational balancing act where girls initiate, adults guide, girls take the reins, and adults respond with support. "[The girls] are writing the petitions, and pushing them out," Campbell says. "They're deciding what they want, and how they are going to ask for it, and then the adults schedule the conference calls, help make that initial professional contact, organization to organization."

Adults also offer support by developing curricular materials that deepen girls' knowledge and skills. At Girls for Gender Equity, Joanne Smith says, "our curriculum brings them through various social justice issues." Topics covered at meetings include "'Identity, Oppression 101,' 'Exploring Race and Racism,' 'Movement Building,' 'Women's History and Waves of Feminism,' and 'Visioning and Collective Power.'[2] This shapes their organizing work as they're developing their lens on activism and why it's important to be an activist and to speak out."

Offering connections and networks is also a powerful means of support. Because of personal history and past experiences, adults have access to helpful connections with people in the community, with other organizations and activists, and with the media and the press. Yas loves that adults at SPARK are so open with their contacts; that they say to her things like, "Do you want Shelby Knox's email? Cause I can give it to you." Izzy agrees. "We don't have connections the adults have." And so it's important to be able to tap into "such a broad network." When I ask Simone what she values in her work with adults at Hardy Girls, she says it's "connecting, networking, and sharing info." She appreciates all the introductions adults make and loves when adults say to her, "I found this article for you." It's important to have someone who knows other people and the terrain and who's willing to pass on to girls the power of this kind of networking. The girls created an amazing action with *Seventeen*, but "there is no way it would have blown up the way it did without Shelby Knox at Change.org," Campbell says. "She had all these contacts!"

It's a powerful thing when adults make full use of their connections in the service of the youth activists they work with. "A lot of the campaigns or the projects are born out of Sisters in Strength's ideas and supported by adults from different organizations and from the adults at Girls for Gender Equity, providing tools, the means and access to theory and resources," Amina Harris explains. By connecting her youth group "to NYQUEER conference organizers," Darla Linville says, she was able to offer an opportunity for her youth researchers to present the data they were gathering and to connect with other queer activists. "Inviting groups like Girls for Gender Equity and SPARK and Stop Street Harassment to my classroom engages students with today's leaders of feminist activism on the ground," says Ileana Jiménez. "As a result, they see the ways in which feminist work manifests itself across different kinds of platforms and visions, leading my students to get involved with these groups both during and after taking my course."

Providing support means offering what girls need in the moment, which requires that adults listen and remain open and flexible. At Girls for Gender Equity, where girls are developing participatory action research projects, "adults organize background support," Brianna says, and, depending on the project, that support looks like meeting space, workshops, rally materials, and transportation to actions and meetings. "Being able to provide them with transportation is important," Harris says, which means picking girls up, offering gas cards or subway or train passes, or, if getting together physically isn't possible, providing online platforms for virtual conversations and meetings. Hardy Girls offers mileage reimbursement when driving makes sense. Safety, especially in the winter, is important to consider. "It was getting harder and harder to ask people to drive two hours one way" for monthly board meetings, Dupont says of a Girls Advisory Board that includes members from various towns in rural Maine. "So we've come up with other ways, like Skype and conference calls, Google Hangouts, too."

Support, when possible, is also financial. SPARK stipends girls as a way to value their contributions as both bloggers and activists. Linville, too, felt it was important to pay the youth researchers she worked with. "I wanted to be able to stipend them for their time. That was a central piece for me, to say, you know, 'You are partners in this, you, your information, your experience is valuable and this is work that you're doing and you should be paid for it.'"

Background support can also look like the most basic necessities. Smith thinks a lot about the kinds of support Girls for Gender Equity offers the high school girls of color in their Sisters in Strength program. She has no use for the distinctions funders typically make between providing shelter or a meal and supporting the girls' in their social-change efforts. After all, having the energy and time for activism requires that girls come to the table unburdened by hunger and concerns for their safety or well-being. Activism is for everybody, and most effective when we meet girls where they are. If we don't, Joanne says, "we're perpetuating the oppression that we're fighting to change."

As Loud as We Want to Be

A safe space, a place for girls to gather and do their work, "a consistent space that is accessible to girls," is essential, Dupont says. The Girls Advisory Board at Hardy Girls meets in the same room the Adult Board meets, for example. Beyond the consistency, however, a space is safe when it allows girls to speak their truths in the ways they need to. Referring to her activist project with queer youth, Linville explains:

> We needed a space where we could be as loud as we wanted to be. That was a necessary condition and one that we didn't have and one that caused a lot of stress for me. We needed a space that was just ours so that when kids were talking about sex or being queer or harassment that had happened to them on the street, people weren't walking by and making frowny faces at them about how they were being inappropriate or using language that they shouldn't be using or saying things that shouldn't be said or behaving in a way that wasn't right. They need a space where they can say whatever they need to say and they don't have to cover up the ugly that is happening to them. The ugly they are experiencing. We needed a space where youth were welcome.

Spaces are safe when adults make room for girls to be themselves, which means they are spaces in which adults have taken seriously what it means to partner with girls, engage in genuine relationship, practice their trustworthiness and loyalty—all those other necessary conditions. A former student of gender and women's studies professor Ruth Nicole Brown writes about the questions she learned to ask when she worked with Brown at SOLHOT, a feminist hip-hop space Brown created "to celebrate Black girl-hood in all of its complexity."[3]

- Why do you need them to be quiet? Why in a free space does their volume need to be at a certain place in order for you to engage with them?
- Why do you have a problem with their sexual freedom? Why do questions about sex, sexuality, pleasure and the politics around those things make you pause? Truly, ask yourself if you can be here for Black girl freedom and still want to police and control their sexualities.
- Why are you there?
- What privileges do you have that they do not have? And don't be surface about the shit. Like truly evaluate all of these things, because it will make you more aware, sensitive and conscious of your positionality in their lives/space. Nothing feels worse than alienating and slighting someone you really are here to support.

Our ability to answer questions about our impulse to contain or control girls we work with is connected directly to the safety of the spaces we offer them and our trustworthiness as adults. "I think that it's important to really check our assumptions," Harris says, "and understand the power dynamics that can exist in a space, even when we're trying to undo them in a space, like acknowledge that and sit with it, let our understanding be transparent as adults."

Work with Me

"Youth are on a different schedule than adults; we have school, sports, clubs, and other activities, and these commitments need to be considered when finding a time to meet," Maya and Treva write in their tip sheet on partnering with girls. Girl after girl reiterates this reality, echoing seventeen-year-old Simone's wish that adults "respect girls' time," and acknowledge that "we might not be adults, but we're just as busy." Instead of assuming girls work around adult schedules, Brianna, fifteen, says, how about adults "try to work with my schedule?" Dupont agrees. "Oftentimes adults don't consider that girls have really busy lives, and so [the Girls Advisory Board] meets on a Sunday afternoon. And there are a lot of adults who are like, 'I don't want to do that, because it's the weekend'; well, that's the best time they can meet." It's true, GGE's Smith says:

> Their schedules are packed in ways that have changed, I think, from twenty years ago. They have planners, and a number of afterschool events that they are accountable to attend. Not only sports, but debate, community service hours, test prep, church functions, work, homework, not to mention gender-specific burdens that require them to support their families like providing childcare to siblings, interpreting for family members at the doctor's office if they don't speak the language, geriatric care, et cetera. Those are some of the biggest challenges contributing to their needs being met.

SPARK's online approach to activism helps to circumvent this problem when it comes to meetings. "You are never going to start a feminist group after school if you have to work every day," Campbell says, "but you could do SPARK because we're much more flexible and because I know your schedule and I know when your other commitments are . . . I can work with you on that." But time and schedule complexities emerge when actions heat up and take off. When SPARK's *Seventeen* magazine campaign began to receive national media attention, both Julia and Izzy found themselves scrambling to make things work in a world of adult schedules. Julia explains:

> I had a lot of opportunities and that's really good, that's really rewarding; I really enjoy that stuff. But sometimes it can get to be kind of a lot, and you often feel, like, pressured when someone

gives you an opportunity; you have to accept it. You feel like super busy, and you have a ton of stuff to do, and we're in high
school; people have homework to do, and it could be kind of
hard to say no and especially to an adult, I think, because you
should feel like, "Wow, I'm so thankful for these opportunities
that they are giving me."

A self-described "super type-A personality person," Izzy's impulse
was to fully jump in too. But it messed with her schoolwork: "Because, like, man. I had to miss like a week of school. And like, why
do they do these things on Wednesday afternoons and not a weekend? 'Cause [they assume] kids don't do activism work and adults
do it, so like all these people plan banquets and award ceremonies
and stuff on like Wednesdays, and I'm like, 'Well, I'm in bio class
right now.'"

Given adult privilege in these circumstances—in intergenerational projects journalists usually contact and make arrangements
through the adults, at least initially—the onus is on the women
activists to ensure they check in with girls and plan schedules together. The *Seventeen* magazine media response was a surprise,
and the aftermath was new for everyone, but while it took some
time and conversation, the adults stepped back and created space
for Izzy and Julia to talk about the stress they felt in the face of so
many offers, and the power to pick and choose, to say yes or no
without consequences. To do otherwise risked using the girls as
tokens for an adult agenda. It also risks burning them out. It's so
important that adults emphasize self-care; that we remind girls to
"make mental health a priority" and ensure that they have "down-
time to recharge," Alice says.

Layers of Support

"To foster the right kind of environment for activism . . . people have to be comfortable with other aspects of their life first,"
Treva says, and so it's really important that adults understand that

"you're going through a lot when you're going through puberty in middle school, with social dynamics and family problems and homework." Joanne Smith agrees. "A big part of supporting girls is supporting them in their youth-development stage, because they are young and still working through circumstances in their lives." This includes appreciating what girls are experiencing in their daily lives that might prevent their involvement, as Smith says, "to be sure that [girls] are not slipping through the cracks as we are developing campaigns." As she works with young women in the Sisters in Strength program, Harris says, "I think about how demanding their lives already are." She often finds herself reflecting on the layers of family and work responsibilities the girls negotiate and how that affects their ability to show up ready to do activist work.

> They're sisters, sometimes; they have to be held accountable to their households, whatever that might look like, whether that may mean paying a utility bill or whether it means making sure you're home in time to cook dinner or watch a younger sibling, or getting homework done, making sure you're in good academic standing, or taking care of a kid. So I think the conditions need to be there for young women to actively, like, create space that meets their needs as well as enables them to do that activist work that they want to do.

"It's disheartening" when those needs aren't met, Smith says, "because it speaks to just not understanding how complicated these issues are."

> You can't expect young people to be social justice activists who work on issues that affect society that we all have been trying to solve for most of our lives, and yet not address the personal needs that they have and what brought them here to engage in system change in the first place. When these young women come to us we have to be able to support them, and we have to be able to support them in a way that they inform us, not just in the

way that we think we should be supporting them. That requires a process of counseling, it requires a process of building trust, and it requires direct service.

These issues *are* complicated, and yet in some ways they are so simple. Obviously, it's a lot harder to create the world you want if you're hungry. You can't give your best self if you feel overwhelmed with responsibilities at home. As Smith says, "You can't go to a rally without a coat." Because young women are chosen for the Sisters in Strength Youth Organizing Program solely on their interest and passion for the work and regardless of their level of need, Girls for Gender Equity commits to providing every girl the layers of support necessary to do the work. A social worker herself, Smith ensures there's always someone in the organization ready and able to respond to the girls' "identity needs, their health needs, their educational needs, their community needs." For Harris, once a member of Sisters in Strength, it's all about "meeting a person where they're at and addressing their needs holistically." This means "one-on-one counseling with a master of social work mentor" for an hour each week "to troubleshoot issues in their lives" and, if they need it, "peer college counseling workshops through their College Access Resource and Action program." It's all about "supporting the girls through whatever it is that they're going through," Smith adds, "so they can make informed decisions [as an activist]," yes, "but also so they can pass the test [at school]." She elaborates:

> The systemic issues that affect girls and women of color and trans or nonconforming youth are the structural issues that maintain the status quo and the power. For us to deconstruct these issues we have to organize and we have to advocate, and so that will always be at the core of work, and at the same time, as long as young people are coming to us to do that, we are going to support them in their development and what it is that they need at that time.

Most of us working with girl activists don't have individual counseling services in place or funds to support girls' health or even to provide basic material needs, but we do have the ability and obligation to look around for the people and organizations that can offer girls the things we can't. If we want all girls to have the experience of social and political engagement that activism affords, we'll create a bigger web of adults in their lives who can work with and support them. In schools this means reaching out to other adults girls trust. These aren't always the people we might expect. A group of rural girls in poverty I worked with over the course of a year sought out the women cafeteria workers in their school for warm drinks and advice when things got tough. I made it my business to know these women. In spite of the "one caring adult" cliché popular in the resiliency literature, girl activists need the proverbial village. One of the best things we can do is help them map that village for supporters and allies.

We can also create opportunities for girls to build relational support with other girls. SPARK welcomes each new girl by assigning her a more experienced SPARK sister, a "person you can go to for anything—questions, insecurities, fears," Alice explains. "It's so comforting." Between strategizing and skill building, Hardy Girls builds important relationship-building time into each monthly Girls Advisory Board meeting, invites the girls to attend different events together, and arranges an annual overnight retreat. Girls for Gender Equity's Sisters in Strength team meets twice a week after school for three hours each time to plan and work together and devotes the last Wednesday of each month to "healthy sisterhood meetings," where the girls "take the reins" and build support "by talking about whatever it is they're going through together."

Thinking Like a Tree

Michael Resnick, professor of learning research at MIT's Media Lab, tells a tale of the "walking tree" found in the rain forests of Costa Rica. The roots of the tree, partially visible, slowly branch out to test the ground for good soil and, once found, dig in. As the roots become stronger, the entire tree slowly shifts in that direction, where new roots grow and take hold.[4] This ecological strategy may not be the most direct or efficient method, Resnick says, but because it relies on "small contributions by (and interactions among) many simple entities (e.g., the roots of the tree), rather than a single, sophisticated decision-making entity," it can be flexible, responsive, and adaptive to local conditions, and produce new solutions.[5]

Knowing what to look for and how to respond to the ebb and flow of different needs in ways that support but don't overpower girls sounds really hard, and it would be if the onus were on us to somehow know in advance how to be and do all these things. Thankfully, in an intergenerational, decentralized enterprise, adults and girls develop ways of working collectively, supporting one another, and problem-solving together. Practice makes all of us more attuned to what's happening around us, more able to reach out and test the soil for possibilities. Studies show that adults who put time into creating such conditions for youth, compared to those who parachute in for the short term, become "ecological thinkers": faced with obstacles and dilemmas, they "see potential not pathology." They become good at anticipating contingencies and they learn how to "balance diverse and competing considerations," even as they keep youth at the center.[6]

Experienced adults don't take over, then; they "make things happen for you," says Simone; "with you," I might add. "The tool I bring is of an activist," Ileana Jiménez says. Adult activists offer a way of thinking and a way of being in relationship to girls and to our work together. We bring big-picture skills and on-the-ground support strategies learned over time. We remain open to the questions, issues, and possibilities we discover together with girls. Jiménez knows that no matter how often she and other adult activists "have fallen on our faces," or how much easier it would be to help girls avoid "the pitfalls and gaps and absences that we know exist because we've gone through them ourselves," that "they need to experience that too." Their experiences, especially their failures, take us all to a different place.

In the end, the best gift adult activists can offer is our power to bring together a varied intergenerational collection of people, knowing a diversity of minds and hearts has the best chance of success. As Dana Edell explains, "It's [girls'] experiences and their ideas and their radar of 'that's cool, that's not cool' that really fuels our work, but then the adults look at the bigger picture." Those who shift their mind-set in this way, from controlling a process to creating the best conditions for full participation, "create fertile environments in which interesting activities and ideas are likely to grow and evolve."[7] Like the wandering tree, if the soil is rich, the roots will dig deep and take hold.

Wicked Problems and Willful Girls

*We have to create; it's the only thing
louder than destruction.*

ANDREA GIBSON, "YELLOWBIRD"

We tell youth in a whole variety of ways that we, as adults, are the arbiters of success and well-being. We act as if the pathways to psychological health, good relationships, and civic responsibility are one-directional—all roads lead to us and what we have created. Success, we remind youth daily, is contingent on their ability to accept and work within the constraints of situations, rules, and norms that we have proffered. But of course we don't have it all together. Just look around. It's not pretty: an environmental crisis, global poverty, racial injustice in all its intersectional forms. We are facing what design theorists describe as wicked problems—widespread, complex, and interconnected, these are problems with no single solution, which tear at the fabric of everyday life and touch each one of us where we live.[1]

"We cannot deny the wickedness of wicked problems," design professor Simon Sadler says. "We cannot detach from their political reality, deny our limited ability to solve them, or encourage hubris where we need humility."[2] Yet this is exactly what we so often do. We ask youth to walk lockstep into our classrooms and programs. We insist that they bank *our* knowledge for *their* future, assimilate to our ways of being, accept the current state of affairs. These are unreasonable requests, a bit crazy, in fact, and they know it. We know it. Tackling wicked problems requires an entirely different way of working—one that invites openness, flexibility, creativity; one that creates space for innovation and playfulness, where we can breathe deeply, fill our lungs with possibilities. Wicked problems are passed down from generation to generation. The solutions we offer are only as good as our ability to work across generations, share what we know, creatively make it up together. So why is there so little political education in schools and community organizations, so few opportunities for youth to question the way things usually go, such little encouragement to imagine new pathways? Why are we obsessed with proper and good and coloring between the lines when clearly what the world needs are places where imagination, dissent, and passionate engagement rule? Why are we asking girls and young women, in particular, to "lean in" to flawed systems—systems that prop up wicked problems—when we all should be "digging deep" to address the conditions that undermine and divide us?[3]

The girls and women activists in this book are testament to the collective power of intergenerational projects as places where girls learn to question, explore, build coalitions, and organize, and in so doing spark social imagination as educator and philosopher Maxine Greene defines it: "the capacity to invent visions of what should be and what might be in our deficient society, on the streets where we live, in our schools."[4] All of the girls engaged in this work are connected to adults and communities. They rely on us in a whole variety of ways—for education, for resources and platforms, for guidance, for emotional support, as sounding boards. It's challenging work, it takes our time and energy; it's often frustrating, and sometimes dangerous; it's also wildly creative and our best chance to address the version of wickedness in front of us.

Intergenerational synergy happens far less often than it could and should, not because girls are lazy or tuned out or obsessed with remaking themselves, but because adults don't step in early enough and don't step up often enough. We benefit from the way things are. We fear giving the impression that we don't know what we are doing. Our adult privileges blind us to the brilliance of the youth all around us. For these and other reasons, we set up barriers of various kinds. We defend and protect our version of events. We pass off convention as reality; we pass down expectations, stereotypes, and assumptions as truth. We excuse thoughtless acts in the name of polite society; we shore up inequitable systems to keep the peace. When we let things go by, pretending not to see, not to hear, we encourage girls to disconnect from what they know and want, which means we all lose the potential of their creative forms of dissent.

Willful Girls

To be willful, race and cultural studies professor Sara Ahmed says, is to refuse "to give way, to give up, to give up your way." Girl activists are willful girls. They have the audacity to interrupt the usual flow of events. "You can feel a force most directly when you attempt to resist it," Ahmed says. "It is the experience of 'coming up against' that is named by willfulness." In these instances, "we might need to be the cause of obstruction. We might need to get in the way if we are to get anywhere."[5] The very best gift we can offer girls is how best to get in the way.

There is a weird disconnect between what we associate with willfulness and what we say we want for girls. Girls leadership programs talk more about helping girls develop "grit" than high self-esteem these days, but the concepts have much in common. Psychologist Angela Duckworth describes grit as "working really hard to make your future a reality."[6] This, of course, is the neoliberal ideal. It's also a way to justify our privilege by blaming those victimized by societal inequities for their lack of "passion and perseverance."[7] There is a fundamental difference between success measured as personal improvement and success measured as compassionate leadership. What we want for girls should have something to do with courage—with speaking up against injustice, with standing against hurt, with becoming a threat to inequity,[8] with getting in the way. That is, it should have something to do with being willful. We should be concerned when it doesn't. As sociologist Julie Bettie warns, "When the accomplishment of middle-class norms is linked to mental health and understood as an individual trait (i.e., this girl has high self-esteem) . . . rather than linked to structural inequalities (i.e., this girl has race and class privileges), it gives cause to question the distinction between having self-esteem and being arrogant," between high self-esteem and "a feeling of cultural superiority."[9]

In my experience, willful girls are likely to call out such arrogance and name such injustices, which means they won't do well in normative or lean-in types of girls leadership programs. In truth, it's a pretty unusual adult who actually wants to spend time with willful girls. Or maybe we do until they say something we don't want to hear, stand for something we might not like, step out of line or over the lines we have drawn. Then they are not easy to be with. Then they are "bad" girls, "at risk" girls; inconvenient truths. What is high self-esteem if it's not reflected in a girl's willful behavior? What do we call all those willful girls who challenge us, who make life a challenge for us? What do we do with them?

All girls are willful girls until they aren't. Until they meet their match—some force that stems the tide of their passionate beliefs and enthusiastic imagination; some barrier between what is and what's possible. Until they are not willful in the ways we value— that is, in the ways that make us feel good, reflect back our good decisions and correct beliefs. Until they challenge us where we live. Then they are the troublemakers in our crosshairs or the girls pushed out or pushed aside.

The willful girls in this book know they are irritants. Like a burr under a saddle, they know they cause discomfort; they are a bother, a disruption, an interruption. When I ask them what advice they would give younger girls interested in activism, they want to prepare them for the experience of being the problem. "There is a lot of backlash in activism work, especially in feminism," Izzy says. "Activism is hard," she adds, but "it's more important to do this work than it is to feel bad." Kaitlin agrees. "You're going to get push-back from the people who benefit from the structure the way that it is." But "don't be afraid to share your opinion," Cheyanne advises young activists. "Whether people think your opinion is right or not doesn't matter." Just "keep fighting," Treva agrees. "You know that when pushback happens it's because the word is getting out there and people are starting to hear what you're saying."

Girls want other girls to know what the barriers look and feel like, to help them anticipate shaming tactics, efforts to shut them down, and the pressure to make amends. It's important to make distinctions, Kaitlin says, between hurting people and dissenting. "When you hurt someone" or when "you tread on people's toes, you want to apologize . . . But that's entirely different from apolo-gizing for your passion, beliefs, for doing what you think is right. Don't apologize when you are right and it was your action. Don't apologize for what you've done. Own up to it and say, 'This is me. Yeah I did this.' Yup, work it."

Activists, the girls tell their imagined young protégés, question what they've been taught and trust what feels wrong or off; they don't accept at face value what others tell them. "Look at things like it's the first time," Montgomery advises. "Look at them like you are from another planet and ask, 'Is that really fair? Or is that right? Do I really think that's right?' If you are raised in our coun-try you will most likely have to rewire a lot of what you've been taught. Read things you wouldn't have read before. Rethink a lot of things. Look at things differently."

In the end, it's worth it to fight for something you believe in. The reality is, Izzy says, "your feelings will get hurt." It will be easier not to care. "But like, keep going and don't stop." When Alice thinks back to her middle-school self, she wants to shout, "Care about stuff! Don't worry so much about being like chill or cool or whatever, which is like, 'Who cares?' Like, give a shit!" In the vernacular of adolescence, "I don't care" can become a protective front against daily indignities, pressures, and open hostilities. But it's also a kind of giving up on curiosity, on passion, on possibilities.

But most of all, the girls say—and this is what makes them so different from TEDified versions of girl activists—don't go it alone. One girl after another advises those younger to find people who share their passions and projects and to find community organizations with adults who will support them. "Find a group," Maya says, "or start a group. Find some people who think the same way as you do. Starting at the community level is the best place because that's where there are people who really care about you." You'll need to be discerning, for sure. You'll need to "listen to your instincts about the people in your life that are good for you," Alice says. You'll want to "distance yourself" from "toxic" people who don't get that "activism is about making change and not collecting personal accolades," Katy says, from people "who treat activism like a competition." But in the end, find your people and "keep each other going," Jasmine advises. Find "other girls and adults who help you" and who "you can rely on." "Get a group," her friend Amber agrees. "Don't try to do it on your own."

So activism is hard, it requires effort and company and a thick skin, but in the end, Yas says, "It is just absolutely the most wonderful thing." Yas has been involved in activism for years—on the SPARKteam, through her efforts in support of comprehensive sex education, and in her work for *Powered by Girl*. More than anything else, Yas wants younger girls to know how personally transformative intergenerational activism can be. "I was confused about my identity, because when I was a kid I wanted to wear boys' clothes," she explains. "I didn't really care. And that didn't change, but I sort of changed because I wanted to fit the ideal of how I thought I should be. You sort of get to a point where you are pressured so much." Becoming a feminist and an activist, Yas said, "I just decided that I don't really care what anybody else really thinks. I kind of do things anyways."

How Not to Be the Wall

There are so many ways to enable girls' activism. Perhaps the hardest thing of all is learning how not to be the wall—how not to interrupt the flow of a child raised conventionally girl who loves boys' clothing. How not to be the force that pushes young Yas toward an ideal that cuts her off from the deepest parts of herself. When I ask the girls what advice they would give women who want to work with and support girl activists, they offer all kinds of ways not to be the wall—"not to dim down the energy and excitement teenage girls have," Simone says. "Not to take control over a lot of things," Ty adds. "Let girls be creative, and have our strong feelings," says Jasmine. Give girls "the opportunity to speak out, and have their opinions heard," advises Yas. The list goes on: "Don't put us down," "be honest," "be a decent person," "show up," "show that you care," "be open," "listen," "check your adult privilege." And then, Yas says, offer hope. Let girls know, she says, that "everybody has the ability to change the world, but we just have to start believing that we do. Breaking down the barriers really, we are all in this together. We are all fighting against the same backlash."

It is good for girls to engage the world critically, to be knowledgeable and aware. It is good for a world rife with wicked problems to have a generation of girls with energy, with passion that hasn't been dispersed, drained, redirected, or fragmented. It is also good for those of us who work with them. Quite simply, Joanne Smith says, working with girls "will make your life better." The women activists in this book have benefited in so many ways from learning to become the adults girls say they want. They have revisited, as Ileana Jiménez says, the "pitfalls and gaps and absences" in their own lives to rediscover the value of openness, of messiness, and they have come to understand, as activist Rebecca Solnit says, that "perfection is a stick with which to beat the possible."[10] Working with girl activists changes us. As girls learn to "give a shit" about some things, women learn not to care so much about others. As girls step into the fray, women learn, as Dana Edell says, to be "brave and not give a fuck when the haters are going to hate." As girls' willfulness reveals the wall, the women they work with learn how to be more porous, open, how to fall away. "Let's face it," Judith Butler says, "we're undone by each other. And if we're not, we're missing something."[11] When we take girls as experts on their own lives we become accountable not just to them, but to ourselves—we who were once young with a different set of choices and possibilities, compromises, roads and roadblocks; we who are still, even as adults, both vulnerable and resistant. Waves of recognition, clarity, uncertainty, risks of knowing and not knowing are part of our undoing. Conversations that bend toward curiosity and humor, confusion and anger, voice and relationship are a kind of unraveling. The potential is in the letting go—of our need to control girls, to persuade, discipline, or determine meaning. In the service of creative solutions and new possibilities, we become unsettled and uncertain.

Girls can get in the way of our enjoyment, our pleasure in working with them. Their responses are enlightening in the ways they reveal tension between girls and women. A good kind of tension, which is not to say an easy one or one that feels good, but rather the kind that comes from a challenge to the ways we see and do things. As they set their own boundaries, we can feel uninvited, pushed out, alienated, out of relationship with those we want most to work with, when we most want to work with them. As they begin to say, "Not now, not this way," we are left with "When then, and how?" They can be our "feminist killjoys," taking away our contentment and happiness, interrupting our flow. But this too is a gift. As Ahmed says, "a killjoy can be a knowledge project, a world-making project."[12] Their persistent rejection of our version of success, of our version of a future, is the best we can hope for.

In the end, our work with girl activists is offering support of many kinds, staying present in the aftermath of less-than-perfect actions, offering loyalty when the powers that be use shame and discipline to dissuade dissent. Respecting girls as a force to be reckoned with is humbling. Respecting boundaries, knowing when we are not helpful, when we are not needed, waiting for direction, speaking when spoken to is incredibly hard. But if we want girls to be able to "fuck up and not have their entire world come crashing down," as Melissa Campbell says, we have to represent the part of the world that stays intact, that can take it, and that believes in them whether or not we agree with them.

Girls are targets of neoliberalism in its most predatory forms: marketers and media seek them out, offering the promise of exceptionality and then profiting from the inevitable insecurities, anxieties, and desires—profiting even from their creative forms of resistance. Girls are touted as the new model citizens, sociologist Jessica Taft argues, but "offered a limited model for engagement—one that is individualized, de-politicized, and rooted in neoliberal notions of personal responsibility."[13] Against this, the intergenerational girl-fueled activism we offer can seem like a drop in the bucket. What are small acts of community protest or online resistance against the vested interests of billion-dollar bank accounts?

But if we are truly in the midst of what educator and cultural critic Henry Giroux calls "a systemic war on the radical imagination,"[14] then intergenerational activist work with girls is absolutely the best way to preserve the local, the grassroots, against the pressures of consumer culture. Our feminist work with girls ensures counterpublic spaces where the creative, the unpredictable, the unmarketable thrive; where girls have control over the way things go, where they can debate what matters, where they can shore up their willfulness.

I'm reminded of a recent exchange I witnessed between students at my college and visiting speaker Patrisse Cullors, cofounder of Black Lives Matter. Black Lives Matter began as a brilliant social media campaign, but Cullors is first and foremost an experienced community organizer. When an undergraduate student of color who aspired to get a job teaching "anywhere but my hometown of Baltimore" asked for advice about getting involved in the movement, Cullors paused thoughtfully. "First, I'd like you to stop and reflect on why you want to leave Baltimore." Her point: We do our best work together if we know what we know, if we stay in relationship, if we learn from one another, if we work together. The hard work, Cullors emphasized, is on the ground, building coalition, working to change existing inequities in the places where we live. Most of the girls I interviewed for this book began their activism in their schools and community organizations, some as young as twelve years old. By the time I interviewed them, they had three, four, even six years of activist experience under their belts. They are now expert in constructive critique, knowledgeable about the manipulations of media, skilled at working together to make the world a more just and caring place. They leave our programs and organizations transformed, ready to seed all kinds of beautiful trouble. This work is an investment of enormous value.

"Knowing, like living, grows up out of the dirt and the cracked pavement—through the fences and around the corners," says educator Noah De Lissovoy. "It reveals itself in uninvited and miraculous shoots that spring up everywhere that people live and struggle. This living knowledge of experimentation and protest, of assertion and critique, ubiquitously presses outward into its surroundings."[15] In girls' hands, we set loose glorious possibilities. Our small, local efforts to scaffold their brilliance moves into the world in all kinds of hopeful ways and in all kinds of creative forms.

It comes down to this. If we want girls who are engaged in our schools and communities, we have to affirm, understand, and invest in the conditions that support them. If we want girls who can grapple with the culture of power in effective and promising ways, we need to share what we know about how the culture works and responds. If we want girls who can bring their entire selves to solving social problems, we need to step into relationships in ways that open up space for creativity and imagination. We need to ask hard questions, support their best thinking about how to open up systems to scrutiny, use our privilege as adults to clear a path, offer our time, our expertise, our connections, our passion, and our belief in what they know—and whatever else it takes to bring their creative solutions into being. And we need to insist on the importance, the visibility, and the benefits of our part in this, because what we learn doing this work is instructive and we need so many more of us doing this work.

This is an urgent call for what Ahmed defines as a "willful politics . . . a collective politics"[16] in the form of intergenerational feminist partnerships. If we want girls to experience, in novelist Jeanette Winterson's words, "an imagination that will detonate life, not decorate it,"[17] we must risk a step into the unknown and "[live] out our hope and resistance in public together."[18] Without a forceful reaction to that which hurts and divides us, this generation of girls will battle a precarious world filled with increasingly wicked problems, armed with little more than neoliberal pablum. Stepping into the difficult work of feminist activism with girls is a complex, radical, boundary-crossing interruption of the way things usually go. It's also wildly creative and vitally necessary if we are to create the world we want and if we are to sustain that world over time.

Acknowledgments

Powered by Girl emerged as a kernel of an idea when I began teaching courses on girl-fueled activism years ago and couldn't find a book that encouraged my students both to step back and read the environment for systemic inequities and step in close to listen and learn from girls about their lives. Personal loss and life transitions caused me to put research on hold for a few years, and so I threw myself into activist work with girls at SPARK Movement and Hardy Girls, and with my students on campus fighting for a living wage for staff, demanding a Gender and Sexual Diversity Resource Center, and organizing the underground EDFC (Emily Dickinson Fight Club) to incite a more critical and more loving community. All the while, I listened and learned and wrote notes to myself. When I finally began this book, I felt thoroughly grounded and in good company.

I hired Ruth Frank-Holcomb, a member of the EDFC, as my research assistant. She has been a true friend on this journey. Thank you, Ruth, for your insight and all the ways you've helped make this book happen. Thanks also to my student Kate Parsons, who spent a summer reading interviews and developing themes with me, and to Sonia Vargas and Emily Berner for much-needed student research assistance.

My good friends kept me sane and whole. Thank you, Sharon Lamb and Betty Sasaki, for long conversations, walks with the dogs, and for reading early drafts. Thank you, Deb Tolman and Dana Edell, for your friendship and for sharing in this outrageous and beautiful vision that is SPARK Movement. So much gratitude to my other SPARK leadership-team members over the years: Amy Castro Baker, Shareeza Bhola, Julie Burton, Melissa Campbell, Shelby Knox, Crystal Ogar, and Jamia Wilson; and, of course, deep love to the entire SPARKteam of incredible girls and young women. You are the most brilliant allies, activists, and friends. Thank you, Hardy Girls peeps Megan Williams, Jackie Dupont, Lynn Cole, Karen Heck, Tobi Schneider, and Anne Belden, for teaching me so much about how to work in coalition. And thank you, Kelli McCannell and Christine Bright, for expertly taking the Hardy Girls reins.

I'm grateful to Colby College's Interdisciplinary Studies Division for funding this project through a series of small grants. Thanks and love to Carol Mann, my super smart agent. And thank you to the dream team at Beacon, especially my editor Joanna Green, who got this book immediately and who is an expert guide. I'm truly grateful to Lacey Louwagie VenOsdel and Emily Bent for reading early drafts and offering such insightful suggestions.

I have had the privilege of living with two beautiful people for a very long time, and I'm grateful every day for their love and support. My partner, Mark Tappan, is without question the most skilled community activist I know and has taught me so much about kindness and tenacity. Our daughter, Maya, grew up with parents who changed pronouns in her storybooks, sent her to school unaware of Cinderella's existence, and talked feminism to her adolescent friends. Thankfully, intergenerational backup from Hardy Girls and SPARK made this all seem perfectly normal. Thank you, Maya, for living this work with me and participating in this project as a SPARKteam and Hardy Girls activist.

Writing this book has been a way to honor the brilliant women and girls—theorists, educators, and activists—I've had the pleasure of learning from and working with. Thank you for doing so much to make this the kind of world we all want to live in.

Resources

Books That Inspire and Activate

Baumgardner, Jennifer, and Amy Richards. *Grassroots: A Field Guide for Feminist Activism*. New York: Farrar, Straus and Giroux, 2005.

Brown, Ruth Nicole. *Hear Our Truths: The Creative Potential of Black Girlhood*. Champaign: University of Illinois Press, 2013.

hooks, bell. *Teaching to Transgress: Education as the Practice of Freedom*. New York: Routledge, 1994.

Lloyd, Rachel. *Girls Like Us: Fighting for a World Where Girls Are Not for Sale, an Activist Finds Her Calling and Heals Herself*. New York: Harper, 2011.

Martin, Courtney. *Do It Anyway: The New Generation of Activists*. Boston: Beacon Press, 2010.

Morega, Cherríe, and Gloria Anzaldúa, editors. *This Bridge Called My Back: Writings By Radical Women of Color*. 4th edition. Albany: State University of New York Press, 2014.

Smith, Joanne, Meghan Huppuch, and Mandy Van Deven. *Hey, Shorty! A Guide to Combating Sexual Harassment and Violence in Schools and on the Streets*. New York: Feminist Press, 2011.

Solnit, Rebecca. *Hope in the Dark: Untold Stories, Wild Possibilities*. New York: Nation Books, 2005.

Taft, Jessica. *Rebel Girls: Youth Activism and Social Change Across the Americas*. New York: New York University Press, 2011.

Trigg, Mary, editor. *Leading the Way: Young Women's Activism for Social Change*. New Brunswick, NJ: Rutgers University Press, 2010.

FOR GIRLS AND YOUNG WOMEN

Adichie, Chimamanda Ngozi. *We Should All Be Feminists*. New York: Anchor Books, 2015.

Darms, Lisa, editor. *The Riot Grrrl Collection*. New York: Feminist Press, 2013.

Favilli, Elena, and Francesca Cavallo. *Goodnight Stories for Rebel Girls*. Los Angeles, CA: Timbuktu Labs, 2016.

Findlen, Barbara. *Listen Up: Voices from the Next Feminist Generation*. New York: Seal Press, 2001.

Hernandez, Daisy, and Bushra Rehman. *Colonize This! Young Women of Color on Today's Feminism.* New York: Seal Press, 2002.

hooks, bell. *Feminism Is for Everybody: Passionate Politics.* Cambridge, MA: South End Press, 2000.

Karnes, Frances A., and Kristen R. Stephens. *Empowered Girls: A Girls' Guide to Positive Activism, Volunteering, and Philanthropy.* Waco, TX: Prufrock Press, 2005.

Martin, Courtney, and Courtney Sullivan. *Click: When We Knew We Were Feminists.* New York: Seal Press, 2010.

Zeilinger, Julie. *A Little F'd Up: Why Feminism Is Not a Dirty Word.* New York: Seal Press, 2012.

FOR YOUNGER GIRLS

Chin-Lee, Cynthia. *Amelia to Zora: Twenty-Six Women Who Changed the World.* Originally 2005. Watertown, MA: Charlesbridge, 2008.

Nagara, Innosanto. *A Is for Activist.* Originally 2012. New York: Triangle Square, 2013.

Schatz, Kate. *Rad American Women A–Z: Rebels, Trailblazers, and Visionaries Who Shaped Our History . . . and Our Future!* San Francisco: City Lights Publishers, 2015.

Documentary Films and Film Organizations

The Education of Shelby Knox. Directed by Rose Rosenblatt and Marion Lipschutz. 2005.

Feminist: Stories From Women's Liberation. Directed by Jennifer Hall Lee. 2013.

Girls Rock!. Directed by Arne Johnson and Shane King. 2008.

Grrrl Love and Revolution: Riot Grrrl NYC. Directed by Abby Moser. 2012.

Makers: Women Who Make America. Directed by Barak Goodman. 2013.

Miss Representation. Directed by Jennifer Siebel Newsom and Kimberlee Acquaro. 2011.

Pussy Riot: A Punk Prayer. Directed by Mike Lerner and Maxim Pozdorovkin.2013.

She's Beautiful When She's Angry. Directed by Mary Dore. 2014.

Very Young Girls. Directed by David Schisgall and Nina Alvarez. 2007.

Wonder Women! The Untold Story of American Superheroines. Directed by Kristy Guevara-Flanagan. 2012.

There are so many more. . . .

Media Education Foundation: http://www.mediaed.org/

Woman's Work: Feminist Documentaries: http://www.imdb.com/list/ls059324934/

Women Make Movies: The Feminist Initiative: http://www.wmm.com/filmcatalog/pages/c745.shtml

Curricula, Resources, and Toolkits

Adams, Maurianne, and Lee Anne Bell, editors. *Teaching for Diversity and Social Justice*. New York: Routledge, 2013.

Advocates for Youth. *Youth Advocates Toolkit*. http://www.advocatesfor youth.org/.

Brown, Lyn Mikel, and Amy Castro Baker. *SPARKing Change, Encouraging Activism*. New York: SPARK Movement, 2012. http://www.spark movement.org/.

Brown, Lyn Mikel, and Mary Madden. *From Adversaries to Allies: A Curriculum for Change*. Waterville, ME: Hardy Girls Healthy Women, 2009. http://www.hardygirlshealthywomen.org/.

Dupont, Jackie, and Lyn Mikel Brown. *Stronger Together: A Strength-Based Elementary Curriculum for Girls*. Waterville, ME: Hardy Girls Healthy Women, 2012. http://www.hardygirlshealthywomen.org/.

Lesko, Wendy Schaetzel. *Catalyst! Successful Strategies to Empower Young Advocates*. Kensington, MD: Youth Activism Project, 2013. www .youthactivismproject.org.

———. *"Knock-Your-Socks-Off": Training Teens to Be Successful Activists! The Complete Guide for Facilitating This 1-2 Hour Workshop*. Kensington, MD: Youth Activism Project, 2004.

———. *Maximum Youth Involvement! The Complete Gameplan for Community Action*. Kensington, MD: Youth Activism Project, 2006.

Maine Youth Action Network. http://www.myan.org.

School Girls Unite. *Activist Gameplan: Put Your Passion Into Action*. Harrisburg, PA: IPV Prevention Council, 2015. http://www.schoolgirlsunite .org.

———. *Girls Gone Activist! Les Filles Deviennent Des Activistes*. Harrisburg, PA: IPV Prevention Council, 2009.

Blogs and Sites That Educate and Empower

BitchMedia: https://bitchmedia.org

The Crunk Feminist Collective: http://www.crunkfeministcollective.com/

Everyday Feminism: http://everydayfeminism.com/

Feminist.com: http://feminist.com/

Feminist Frequency: http://feministfrequency.com/

Feministe: http://www.feministe.us/blog/

Feministing: http://feministing.com/

Finally Feminism 101: https://finallyfeminism101.wordpress.com/

The Freechild Project: https://freechild.org/

Guerrilla Girls: http://www.guerrillagirls.com/

Ms. Magazine Blog: http://msmagazine.com/blog/

Racialicious: http://racialicious.tumblr.com/

Shaping Youth: http://www.shapingyouth.org/

Sociological Images: https://thesocietypages.org/socimages/
Women, Action & the Media: http://www.womenactionmedia.org/
Women's Media Center: http://www.womensmediacenter.com/

FOR AND BY GIRLS AND YOUNG WOMEN
About-Face: http://www.about-face.org/
FBomb: http://thefbomb.org/
F to the Third Power: https://ftothethirdpower.com/
New Moon Girls: http://www.newmoon.com/
Powered by Girl: http://www.poweredbygirl.org/
Rookie: http://www.rookiemag.com/
Scarleteen: http://www.scarleteen.com/
SPARK Movement: http://www.sparkmovement.org
Teen Voices: https://teenvoicesmagazine.wordpress.com/

Some Transformative Girl-Serving Orgs
About-Face: http://www.about-face.org/
Girls for a Change: http://www.girlsforachange.org/
Girls for Gender Equity: http://www.ggenyc.org/
Girls Leadership Institute: http://www.girlsleadershipinstitute.org/
Girls Rock Camp Alliance: http://girlsrockcampalliance.org/
Hardy Girls Healthy Women: http://www.hghw.org/
The Line Campaign: http://whereisyourline.org/
Ma'yan: http://www.mayan.org/
Project Girl: http://www.projectgirl.org/
School Girls Unite: http://www.schoolgirlsunite.org
SPARK Movement: http://www.sparksummit.com/
viBe Theater Experience: http://vibetheater.org/2010/

Classroom Resources
Education for Liberation Network: http://www.edliberation.org/
Facing History and Ourselves: https://www.facinghistory.org
Feminist Teacher: https://feministteacher.com/
Making Caring Common: http://mcc.gse.harvard.edu/
Rethinking Schools: http://www.rethinkingschools.org/
Teaching for Change: https://www.teachingforchange.org/
Teaching Tolerance: http://www.tolerance.org
Zinn Education Project, Teaching *A People's History*: http://zinnedproject.org

Notes

INTRODUCTION: DIGGING DEEP

1. Wendy Hesford, "The Malala Effect," *JAC: A Journal of Rhetoric, Culture & Politics* 34, no. 1–2 (2014): 142.

2. Anita Harris, "Jamming Girl Culture: Young Women and Consumer Citizenship," in *All About the Girl: Culture, Power, and Identity,* ed. Anita Harris (New York: Routledge, 2004), 167.

3. Ruth Williams, "'Eat, Pray, Love': Producing the Female Neoliberal Spiritual Subject," *Journal of Popular Culture* 3, no. 2 (2001): 613–33.

4. Jessica Pressler, "Lena Dunham the Activist," *Elle,* January 27, 2015, http://www.elle.com/culture/celebrities/a26409/lena-dunham-profile/.

5. Elizabeth Denton, "Transgender Teen Activist Jazz Jennings on Struggling to Fit In and Finding the Courage to Be YOU," *Seventeen,* March 12, 2015, http://www.seventeen.com/celebrity/a29184/transgender-teen-activist-jazz-jennings-will-inspire-you-to-be-your-true-self/.

6. Judith Ohikuare, "Meet the Women Who Created #BlackLivesMatter," *Cosmopolitan,* October 17, 2015, http://www.cosmopolitan.com /entertainment/a47842/the-women-behind-blacklivesmatter/.

7. Marnina Gonick, "Between 'Girl Power' and 'Reviving Ophelia': Constituting the Neoliberal Girl Subject," *NWSA Journal* 18, no. 2 (2006): 11.

8. Ibid., 2.

9. Ibid., 11.

10. Dr. Red Chidgey, review of *Future Girl: Young Women in the Twenty-First Century,* by Anita Harris, *Feminist Media, Memory, Activism* (blog), October 5, 2010, http://feministmemory.wordpress.com/2010/10/05 /future-girl/.

11. Natalie Baker, "Is 'Girl-Power' Advertising Doing Any Good?," Bitch-Media, July 28, 2014, http://bitchmedia.org/post/is-girl-power -advertising-doing-any-good.

12. Sheryl Sandberg, *Lean In: Women, Work, and the Will to Lead* (New York: Knopf, 2013).

13. Tyanna Slobe does a provocative sociolinguistic analysis of what she calls "Mock White Girl" in popular media. In "Mock White Girl and the Trivialization of New Media Solidarity" (a presentation at National

Women's Studies Association Annual Conference, San Juan, Puerto Rico, November 14, 2014), Slobe examined the way media parodies the expressive behaviors of white female adolescents by attributing vapidity to their speech patterns and trivializing the group solidarity generated through girls' use of social media.

14. bell hooks, "Dig Deep: Beyond Lean In," Feminist Wire, October 28, 2013, http://www.thefeministwire.com/2013/10/17973/. Hooks is referring to Angela McRobbie, The Aftermath of Feminism: Gender, Culture, and Social Change (London: Sage, 2009).

15. Leah Lowe, "Toward 'Critical Generosity': Developing Student Audiences," Theatre Topics 17, no. 2 (September 2007): 141–51.

16. In her book, Reviving Ophelia: Saving the Selves of Adolescent Girls (New York: Random House, 1994), Mary Pipher represents girls as "saplings in a storm" of a dangerous "girl poisoning" culture. The book spawned girl-serving programs across the country designed to shore up girls' flagging self-esteem, functioning, in effect, to "fix" girls instead of addressing the conditions that serve to constrain, restrict, and subordinate them.

PART ONE: CULTIVATING DISSENT

1. Sara Corbett, "Enemies of the State," Vogue, June 30, 2014, http://www.vogue.com/946500/pussy-riot-members-start-new-organization-zona-prava/#1.

2. Jessica Zychowicz, "Pussy Riot Arrest at Sochi Reinforces Their Cult Status," Conversation, February 19, 2014, http://theconversation.com/pussy-riot-arrest-at-sochi-reinforces-their-cult-status-23277. Indeed, unmasked and now celebrities in the West, Masha Alekhina and Nadya Tolokonnikova have left Pussy Riot, affirming, as a current group member said, "We are against commercialisation, and we don't want Pussy Riot to become a brand . . . we are still a group with no commercial goal."

3. "And with This Caption Vogue Reminds Us What Really Matters," Mamamia, July 1, 2014, http://www.mamamia.com.au/vogue-pussy-riot-photo-caption/.

4. Ashley Lutz, "These 6 Corporations Control 90% of the Media in America," Business Insider, June 14, 2012, http://www.businessinsider.com/these-6-corporations-control-90-of-the-media-in-america-2012-6.

5. Heather Switzer, "(Post)Feminist Development Fables: The Girl Effect and the Production of Sexual Subjects," Feminist Theory 14, no. 3 (2013): 345–60.

6. Herbert Kohl, "The Politics of Children's Literature: What's Wrong with the Rosa Parks Myth," Zinn Education Project, http://zinnedproject.org/materials/politics-of-childrens-literature-rosa-parks-myth/, accessed April 1, 2016.

7. bell hooks, *Teaching to Transgress: Education as the Practice of Freedom* (New York: Routledge, 1994), 186.

8. Carly Stasko, "(r)Evolutionary Healing: Jamming with Culture and Shifting the Power," in *Next Wave Cultures: Feminism, Subcultures, Activism*, ed. Anita Harris (New York: Routledge, 2008), 193.

CHAPTER ONE: THE MYTH OF THE SPECIAL GIRL

1. *Seventeen* issued its Body Peace Treaty in the August 2012 issue.

2. Elizabeth Snead, *Hollywood Reporter/Billboard*, July 5, 2012.

3. Lauren Torrisi, ABC News, *Good Morning America*, July 5, 2012.

4. Deborah L. Tolman, "SPARKing Change: Not Just One Girl at a Time," *Huffington Post*, May 10, 2012, http://www.huffingtonpost.com/deborah -l-tolman/sparking-change-not-just-_b_1506433.html.

5. Psychologist Deborah Tolman and I cofounded SPARK as a movement to challenge the sexualization of girls in the media, inspired by the American Psychological Association's Task Force on the Sexualization of Girls (Washington, DC: APA, 2007), http://www.apa.org/pi/women /programs/girls/report.aspx. Over time, the girls we worked with—over sixty-five girls and young women from across the United States and from eight other countries—widened our focus beyond sexualization to gender justice.

6. Laura Zegel, "Don't Photoshop My Story!: An Interview with Julia Bluhm," Viral Media Lab, October 28, 2012, http://theviralmedialab .org/5631/2012/10/dont-photoshop-my-story-an-interview-with -julia-bluhm/.

7. Maxine Greene, "Imagination and the Healing Arts," 2007, Maxine Greene Center for Aesthetic Education and Social Imagination, http:// maxinegreene.org/uploads/library/imagination_ha.pdf, 1.

8. Jamia Wilson is now executive director at Women, Action, and the Media (WAM!).

9. Zegel, "Don't Photoshop My Story!," http://theviralmedialab.org/5631 /2012/10/dont-photoshop-my-story-an-interview-with-julia-bluhm/.

10. Tolman, "SPARKing Change," http://www.huffingtonpost.com /deborah-l-tolman/sparking-change-not-just-_b_1506433.html.

11. Courtney Martin, *Do It Anyway: The Next Generation of Activists* (Boston: Beacon Press, 2010), 168.

12. Anita Harris, *Future Girl: Young Women in the Twenty-First Century* (New York: Routledge, 2004).

13. "How Small Town Jersey Girls Sparked a National Debate," Thirteen.org, August 10, 2012, http://www.thirteen.org/metrofocus/2012/08/how-small -town-jersey-girls-sparked-a-national-debate/.

14. Simon Sadler, "TEDification Versus Edification," *Places Journal* (January 2014), http://placesjournal.org/article/tedification-versus-edification/.

15. McKenna Pope, "Want to Be an Activist? Start with Your Toys," November 2013, https://www.ted.com/talks/mckenna_pope_want_to_be _an_activist_start_with_your_toys?language=en.
16. Emma Axelrod at TEDxYOUTH@Hewitt, TED, November 2012, http:// tedxtalks.ted.com/video/TEDxYouthHewitt-Emma-Axelrod.
17. Maya Penn, "Meet a Young Entrepreneur, Cartoonist, Designer, Activist," TED, December 2013, https://www.ted.com/talks/maya_penn_meet_a _young_entrepreneur_cartoonist_designer_activist?language=en3.
18. Emily Bent, "A Different Girl Effect: Producing Political Girlhoods in the 'Invest in Girls' Climate," in *Youth Engagement: The Civic-Political Lives of Children and Youth*, vol. 16 of Sociological Studies of Children and Youth, ed. Sandi Kawecka Nenga and Jessica K. Taft (Bingley, UK: Emerald Group Publishing, 2013), 6.
19. A number of theorists have made the case that girls are increasingly seen as model neoliberal citizens: ibid.; Jessica Taft, "The Political Lives of Girls," *Sociology Compass* 8, no. 3 (2014): 259–67; Gonick, "Between 'Girl Power' and 'Reviving Ophelia.'"
20. George Lipsitz, *The Possessive Investment in Whiteness: How White People Profit from Identity Politics* (Philadelphia: Temple University Press, 1998), 369.
21. Hava Rachel Gordon, "Gendered Paths to Teenage Political Participation: Parental Power, Civic Mobility, and Youth Activism," *Gender & Society* 22, no. 1 (2008): 31–55.
22. Jessica Taft, "Girl Power Politics: Pop Culture Barriers and Organizational Resistance," in *All About the Girl: Culture, Power, and Identity*, ed. Anita Harris (New York: Routledge, 2004), 69–77.
23. Chimamanda Ngozi Adichie, "The Danger of a Single Story," TEDGlobal 2009, http://www.ted.com/talks/chimamanda_adichie_the_danger_of _a_single_story?language=en.
24. Girl Effect, http://www.girleffect.org/.
25. Bent, "A Different Girl Effect," 11.
26. Ibid.
27. "Rachel Parent Debates Kevin O'Leary About GMOs," http://www .huffingtonpost.ca/2013/08/01/rachel-parent-kevin-oleary-gmos-video _n_3689126.html.
28. Jessica Taft, "The Political Lives of Girls," *Sociology Compass* 8, no. 3 (2014): 259–67.
29. Henry A. Giroux, "Protesting Youth in an Age of Neoliberal Savagery," E-International Relations, May 20, 2014, http://www.e-ir.info/2014/05 /20/protesting-youth-in-an-age-of-neoliberal-savagery/.
30. Greene, "Imagination and the Healing Arts," 3.
31. Jessica Taft, *Rebel Girls: Youth Activism and Social Change Across the Americas* (New York: New York University Press, 2011), 43.

32. "Why Sell Thin Mints When You Could Be Starting a Revolution?," MetaFilter, January 22, 2015, http://www.metafilter.com/146376/Why -sell-Thin-Mints-when-you-could-be-starting-a-revolution.

33. "Cofounder Chat: Radical Brownies," "http://www.dropbox.com/s /fuw8fja6opl3ngm/Rad%20Brownies%20Chat%20Updated.mp4?dl=0; Radical Monarchs Community, Facebook, http://www.facebook.com /pages/Radical-Brownies/875969742435827.

34. Robert Montenegro, "'Radical Brownies' Merges Scouting with Social Justice," *Big Think*, http://bigthink.com/ideafeed/radical-brownies -marries-scouting-with-racial-inequality.

35. In *Bodies That Matter: On the Discursive Limits of "Sex"* (New York: Routledge, 1993), Judith Butler theorizes that discourse gains the authority and power to bring about what it names through repetition. I am suggesting adults support resistance to constraining norms through repetition of activist discourses.

36. Taft, *Rebel Girls*, 48.

CHAPTER TWO: EVERYDAY REBELLIONS

1. Sandberg, *Lean In*.

2. Jessica Taft, "Girlhood in Action: Contemporary US Girls' Organizations and the Public Sphere," *Girlhood Studies* 3, no. 2 (2010): 11–29.

3. Ibid., 24. See also Hava R. Gordon and Jessica K. Taft, "Rethinking Youth Political Socialization: Teenage Activists Talk Back," *Youth & Society* 43, no. 4 (2011): 1499–1527.

4. Emily Bent, "'Making It Up': Intergenerational Activism and the Ethics of Empowering Girls," *Girlhood Studies*, forthcoming.

5. Bernice Johnson Reagon, "Coalition Politics: Turning the Century," in *Home Girls: A Black Feminist Anthology*, ed. Barbara Smith (New York: Kitchen Table Press, 1983).

6. Shawn Ginwright, Pedro Noguera, and Julio Cammarota, *Beyond Resistance! Youth Activism and Community Change* (New York: Routledge, 2006), xiii.

7. Lyn Mikel Brown and Carol Gilligan, *Meeting at the Crossroads: Women's Psychology and Girls' Development* (Cambridge, MA: Harvard University Press, 1992); Jill McLean Taylor, Carol Gilligan, and Amy Sullivan, *Between Voice and Silence: Women and Girls, Race and Relationships* (Cambridge, MA: Harvard University Press, 1995); Annie Rogers, "Voice, Play, and a Practice of Ordinary Courage in Girls' and Women's Lives," *Harvard Educational Review* 63, no. 3 (1993): 265–96.

8. Taft, *Rebel Girls*, 149–50.

9. This is a consistent finding of a series of research studies; see, for example, Lyn Mikel Brown, *Girlfighting: Betrayal and Rejection Among Girls* (New York: New York University Press, 2003); Brown and Gilligan,

Meeting at the Crossroads; Taylor, Gilligan, and Sullivan, *Between Voice and Silence*; Deborah L. Tolman, *Doing Desire* (Cambridge, MA: Harvard University Press, 2002).

10. bell hooks, *Teaching Critical Thinking* (New York: Routledge, 2010), 7.

11. Brown and Gilligan, *Meeting at the Crossroads*.

12. Annie Rogers, "Voice, Play, and a Practice of Ordinary Courage in Girls' and Women's Lives," *Harvard Educational Review* 63, no. 3 (1993): 272.

13. Erik Erikson, *Identity, Youth and Crisis* (orig. 1968; New York: Norton, 1994), 258.

14. Aimee Meredith Cox, *Shapeshifters: Black Girls and the Choreography of Citizenship* (Durham, NC: Duke University Press, 2015), 12.

15. Ibid., 10.

16. Ibid.

17. Signithia Fordham, "Those Loud Black Girls": (Black) Women, Silences, and Gender 'Passing' in the Academy," *Anthropology and Education Quarterly* 24 (1993): 3–32.

18. Edward Morris, "'Ladies' or 'Loudies'? Perceptions and Experiences of Black Girls in Classrooms," *Youth & Society* 38, no. 4 (2007): 505–6.

19. Lyn Mikel Brown, *Raising Their Voices: The Politics of Girls' Anger* (Cambridge, MA: Harvard University Press, 1998).

20. Venus Evans-Winters, Brittany Brathwaite, and Fariha Farzana, "Dangerous Bodies: Girls of Color and Harsh Discipline Policies in Schools" (workshop presented at the National Women's Studies Association, Milwaukee, WI, November 13, 2015).

21. Taft, *Rebel Girls*, 91.

22. Adrienne Rich, "Vesuvius at Home: The Power of Emily Dickinson," in her *On Lies, Secrets, and Silence: Selected Prose, 1966–1978* (New York: Norton, 1979), 157.

23. In her article "'I'll Resist with Every Inch and Every Breath': Girls and Zine Making as a Form of Resistance" (*Youth and Society* 35, no. 1 [2003]), Kristen Schilt uses the term *c/overt* to describe resistance that is overtly expressed only to like-minded and trusted others; with respect to untrustworthy authority figures such resistance remains strategically covert and anonymous.

24. hooks, *Teaching Critical Thinking*, 8.

25. James C. Scott, *Domination and the Arts of Resistance: Hidden Transcripts* (New Haven, CT: Yale University Press, 1992).

26. Andrea Gibson, "A Letter to the Playground Bully," track 3 of *Flower Boy*, compact disk, released November 15, 2011.

27. Brown and Gilligan, *Meeting at the Crossroads*, 60.

28. Judith Butler, *Precarious Life: The Powers of Mourning and Violence* (London: Verso 2006), xix.

29. Don Merten, "The Meaning of Meanness: Popularity, Competition, and Conflict Among Junior High School Girls," *Sociology of Education* 70, no. 3 (1997): 175.

30. Carol Gilligan, "Joining the Resistance: Psychology, Politics, Girls, and Women," *Michigan Quarterly Review* 29 (1990): 511.

31. Laina Y. Bay-Cheng and Amanda E. Lewis, "Our 'Ideal Girl': Prescriptions of Female Adolescent Sexuality in a Feminist Mentorship Program," *Affilia* 21 (Spring 2006): 171–83; Laina Y. Bay-Cheng et al., "Disciplining 'Girl Talk': The Paradox of Empowerment in a Feminist Mentorship Program," *Journal of Human Behavior in the Social Environment* 13, no. 2 (2006): 73–92.

32. Joanne Smith, Mandy Van Deven, and Meghan Huppuch, *Hey Shorty! A Guide to Combating Sexual Harassment and Violence in Schools and on the Streets* (New York: Feminist Press, 2011), 11.

33. Butler, *Precarious Life*, 18.

34. Amy Sullivan, "From Mentor to Muse: Recasting the Role of Women in Relationship with Urban Adolescent Girls," in *Urban Girls: Resisting Stereotypes, Creating Identities*, ed. Bonnie Leadbeater and Niobe Way (New York: New York University Press, 1996), 246.

35. Ibid., 244.

36. Ruth Nicole Brown, "Mentoring on the Borderlands: Creating Empowering Connections Between Adolescent Girls and Young Women Volunteers," *Human Architecture: Journal of the Sociology of Self-Knowledge* 4, no. 3 (2006): 110.

37. Bent, "'Making It Up': Intergenerational Activism."

38. Janie Victoria Ward, *The Skin We're In: Teaching Our Children to Be Emotionally Strong, Socially Smart, and Spiritually Connected* (New York: Free Press, 2000).

39. Shawn Ginwright, "Peace Out to Revolution! Activism Among African American Youth: An Argument For Radical Healing," *Young* 18, no. 1 (2010): 82.

CHAPTER THREE: ACTIVISM IS GOOD FOR (ALL) GIRLS

1. Elizabeth Debold, Susan Weseen, Geraldine Kearse-Brookins, and I articulate what we mean by hardiness zones in an article we wrote critiquing resilience theory: "Cultivating Hardiness Zones for Adolescent Girls: A Reconceptualization of Resilience in Relationships with Caring Adults," in *Beyond Appearances: A New Look at Adolescent Girls*, ed. Norine Johnson, Michael Roberts, and Judith Worell (Washington, DC: American Psychological Association, 1999): 181–204.

2. Nancy Fraser, "Rethinking the Public Sphere," in *The Phantom Public Sphere*, edited by Bruce Robbins (Minneapolis: University of Minnesota Press, 1993).

3. I have written about my disdain for the ways popular "bully prevention" programs have effaced real differences that affect young people's lives, distracted from systemic inequities, and even eroded students' rights (see, for example, "10 Ways to Move Beyond Bully Prevention (and Why We Should)" in *Education Week*, March 5, 2008, http://www.edweek.org /ew/articles/2008/03/05/26brown.h27.html; reprinted in *Rethinking Schools* and other publications). *Bullying* is a generic term that de-genders, de-races, de-everythings school safety. It is, however, a term that can be used strategically to get in the school door and do the deeper work with youth and staff not offered by popular bully-prevention programs.

4. Nan Stein and Lisa Sjostrom, *Flirting or Hurting? A Teacher's Guide on Student-to-Student Sexual Harassment in Schools for Grades 6 through 12* (Wellesley, MA: Wellesley College Center for Research on Women, 1994). Nan Stein is a senior research scientist at Wellesley's Center for Research on Women.

5. Greene, "Imagination and the Healing Arts."

6. Courtney E. Martin, "Do It Anyway: The Top 10 Ways That the Next Generation Is Shifting Activism," *Huffington Post*, September 7, 2010, http://www.huffingtonpost.com/courtney-e-martin-/do-it-anyway-the -top-ten-_b_707074.html.

7. To adapt an argument sociologist Barbara Hudson made years ago in her article "Femininity and Adolescence," in *Gender and Generation*, ed. Angela McRobbie and Mica Nava (New York: Macmillan, 1984).

8. Taft, *Rebel Girls*, 90.

9. Ibid.

10. Fordham, "Those Loud Black Girls."

11. D. L. Tolman et al., "Looking Good, Sounding Good: Femininity Ideology and Adolescent Girls' Mental Health," *Psychology of Women Quarterly* 30 (2006): 85–95; American Psychological Association, *Report of the APA Task Force on the Sexualization of Girls* (Washington, DC: APA, 2007), http:// www.apa.org/pi/women/programs/girls/report-summary.pdf.

12. Shelly Grabe and Janet Shibley Hyde, "Body Objectification, MTV, and Psychological Outcomes Among Female Adolescents," *Journal of Applied Social Psychology* 39, no. 12 (2009): 2840–58.

13. Sarah J. McKenney and Rebecca S. Bigler, "High Heels, Low Grades: Internalized Sexualization and Academic Orientation Among Adolescent Girls," *Journal of Research on Adolescence* 26, no. 1 (2016): 30–36, originally published online October 27, 2014, doi:10.1111/jora.12179.

14. Rachel Calogero, "Objects Don't Object: Evidence That Self-Objectification Disrupts Women's Social Activism," *Psychological Science* 24, no. 3 (2013): 312–18, originally published online January 22, 2013, doi:10.1177/0956797612452574.

15. Rachel Simmons, *The Curse of the Good Girl* (New York: Penguin, 2009).

16. Brown, *Raising Their Voices.*

17. Peter Lyman, "The Politics of Anger: On Silence, Ressentiment, and Political Speech," *Socialist Review* 11, no. 3 (1981): 61; Carol Gilligan, "Joining the Resistance," 527.
18. Elizabeth Spelman, "Anger and Insubordination," in *Women, Knowledge, and Reality: Explorations in Feminist Philosophy*, ed. Ann Garry and Marilyn Pearsall (Boston: Unwin Hyman, 1989), 272.
19. Adichie, "The Danger of a Single Story."
20. Lisa Delpit, *Other People's Children: Cultural Conflict in the Classroom* (New York: New Press, 1995), 25.
21. Catherine Snowe, "First, Drop What Doesn't Work," in What Works in Education: Let the Discussion Begin, *Oberlin Alumni Magazine* 107, no. 1 (Winter 2012): 18.
22. Edmund Gordon, Beatrice Bridglall, and Aundra Meroe, *Supplementary Education: The Hidden Curriculum of High Academic Achievement* (Lanham, MD: Rowman & Littlefield, 2005).
23. Ibid.
24. Ibid., 30.
25. Jeff Howard, "You Can't Get There from Here: The Need For a New Logic in Education Reform," *Daedalus: Journal of the American Academy of Arts and Sciences* 124 no. 4 (1995): 85–92.
26. James Coleman, *Equality of Educational Opportunity* (Washington, DC: US Government Printing Office, 1966).
27. Cynthia Taines, "Intervening in Alienation: The Outcomes for Urban Youth of Participating in School Activism," *American Educational Research Journal* 49, no. 1 (2012): 53–86.
28. Ibid., 54.
29. Sinikka Aapola, Marnina Gonick, and Anita Harris, *Young Femininity* (New York: Palgrave Macmillan, 2005); Taft, *Rebel Girls*.
30. Jessica Valenti, "The Upside of Ugly," *Nation*, August 2, 2012, www.thenation.com/blog/169208/upside-ugly.
31. Julie Bettie, *Women Without Class: Girls, Race, and Identity* (Oakland: University of California Press, 2014).
32. Janis Whitlock, *Places to Be and Places to Belong: Youth Connectedness in School and Community* (Ithaca, NY: ACT for Youth Center of Excellence, 2004), 58.
33. Adrienne Rich, "Disloyal to Civilization: Feminism, Racism, Gynephobia," in her *On Lies, Secrets, and Silence* (New York: Norton, 1979), 279.
34. Taft, *Rebel Girls*, 64.
35. Ibid., 68.

PART TWO: NECESSARY CONDITIONS

1. Taft, *Rebel Girls*, 186.
2. Harry Shier, "What Does 'Equality' Mean for Children in Relation to Adults?," background paper for UN global thematic consultation

"Addressing Inequalities Post 2015," October 2012, available at the website of World We Want 2030, https://www.worldwewant2030.org/node/284010.

3. *Mansplaining* is defined as an attempt to explain something to someone (typically an overconfident man to a well-informed woman) in a patronizing way.

4. Taft, "Girlhood in Action," 12.

5. Please see the resources section for detailed demographics on the girls and women activists whose stories make up part 2. I am indebted to my research assistants, Ruth Frank Holcomb and Kate Parsons, who offered invaluable support and insight in shaping this section. Ruth and I together interviewed the girls and women activists, and Ruth and Kate helped me read through the transcripts and develop the organizing themes that became our "necessary conditions."

6. Bent, "'Making It Up': Intergenerational Activism."

7. Greene, "Imagination and the Healing Arts."

8. Bent, "'Making It Up': Intergenerational Activism."

9. Reagon, "Coalition Politics," 365.

CHAPTER 4: BEYOND GLORIA STEINEM

1. Dominique Christina and Denice Frohman, "No Child Left Behind," http://buttonpoetry.tumblr.com/post/89404740489/dominique-christina -denice-frohman-no-child.

2. Comedy Central, *Drunk History*, http://www.cc.com/shows/drunk-history.

3. Howard Zinn, *A People's History of the United States* (New York: Harper Perennial, 2005); see also Zinn Education Project, http://zinned project.org/.

4. "Peggy McIntosh, Founder," National Seed Project, http://nationalseed project.org/59-seed-directors/18-peggy-mcintosh.

5. "About the Zinn Education Project," Zinn Education Project, http:// zinnedproject.org.

6. *Powered By Girl* (poweredbygirl.org) is an online magazine written by girls, for girls. I first started the magazine with the Girls Advisory Board at Hardy Girls, but it has become its own project. I work with Yas and the girl bloggers on a private Facebook group, helping only when asked.

7. Taft, *Rebel Girls*, p. 185.

8. Jiménez's students share their activism in the blog *F to the Third Power*, http://ftothethirdpower.com.

9. Shelby's activism was documented in the 2005 film *The Education of Shelby Knox*, itself a wonderful story of girl activism to share with girls and young women.

10. Radical Women's History Project, http://radicalwomen.tumblr.com.

11. "Spotlight On: Shelby Knox," SheRights, http://sherights.com/2011/02/28 /spotlight-on-shelby-knox/.

12. A sample interview, conducted by SPARKteam member April, who interviewed her friends about women who have inspired them, can be viewed on YouTube: "SPARK Women's History Year–April," http://www.youtube.com/watch?v=TXwjCJ1uGeE.

13. Joneka Percentie, "Black Women Create: Highlighting Black Women in Film and TV," SPARK Movement, March 4, 2014, http://www.spark summit.com/2014/03/04/black-women-create-highlighting-black -women-in-film-and-tv/.

14. Joneka Percentie, Katy Ma, and Aviv Rau, "SPARK Puts Women on the Map!," SPARK Movement, March 2, 2015, http://www.sparksummit .com/2015/03/02/spark-puts-women-on-the-map/.

15. SPARK Movement blog, http://www.sparksummit.com/category/blog/.

CHAPTER FIVE: GOOD INTENTIONS AREN'T ENOUGH

1. Ruth Nicole Brown, "Mentoring on the Borderlands: Creating Empow- ering Connections Between Adolescent Girls and Young Women Volun- teers," *Human Architecture: Journal of the Sociology of Self-Knowledge* 4, no. 3 (2006): 105–21.

2. Bent, "'Making It Up': Intergenerational Activism."

3. Bay-Cheng et al., "Disciplining 'Girl Talk.'" The researchers usefully cri- tique these differences in the conceptualization of power and why they are so important to interrogate in group work with girls.

4. Sullivan, "From Mentor to Muse," 243.

CHAPTER SIX: EXPERTS ON THEIR OWN EXPERIENCE

1. The Bechdel test or Bechdel-Wallace test, made famous by Alison Bechdel in her cartoon strip *Dykes to Watch Out For*, asks whether a film or other creative work has at least two women who talk with each other about something other than a man.

2. Roger Hart, *Children's Participation: The Theory and Practice of Involv- ing Young Citizens in Community Development and Environmental Care* (Florence, Italy: UNICEF, 1992), http://www.unicef-irc.org/publications /100. For a description of Hart's ladder of participation, see "What Does Participation Mean?," MIT Media Lab, http://llk.media.mit.edu/courses /readings/participation-ladder.pdf.

3. *Wikipedia* offers a description of the incident, adult public reaction, and sentencing: "Steubenville High School Rape Case," http://en.wikipedia .org/wiki/Steubenville_High_School_rape_case

4. Rios is a vocal online activist who now writes for Autostraddle. At the time of the action, she was the director of American University's Wom- en's Initiative. Clancy was a member of Mules Against Violence (MAV) at Colby, a group of male athletes doing peer-to-peer sexual-violence -prevention training on campus.

5. The coalition included Ohio Alliance to End Sexual Violence, Futures Without Violence, Mentors in Violence Prevention, California Coalition Against Sexual Assault, National Sexual Violence Resource Center, and the Pennsylvania Coalition Against Rape. See Carmen Rios, "SPARK Is Working with NFHS to #EducateCoaches and Prevent Sexual Violence," SPARK Movement blog, May 8, 2013, http://www.sparksummit.com /2013/05/08/spark-partners-with-nfhs-to-educatecoaches-prevent -sexual-violence/.

6. The participatory action research framework Linville uses arose in collaboration with other researchers at the Graduate Center of the City University of New York (CUNY), such as Michelle Fine, Eve Tuck, Patricia Krueger, Mayida Zaal, Jessica Ruglis, Jen Ayala, and Monique Guishard. For more information on the framework see the Public Science Project website, http://publicscienceproject.org/about/history/.

CHAPTER SEVEN: WIDE AWAKE AND CALLING BS

1. hooks, *Teaching Critical Thinking*, 7.

2. Ibid., 10.

3. Henry Giroux, *Teachers as Intellectuals: Toward a Critical Pedagogy of Learning* (New York: Praeger, 1988), 177.

4. Paulo Freire, *Pedagogy of the Oppressed* (New York: Continuum, 1970).

5. Kimberlé Williams Crenshaw and Andrea J. Ritchie, *Say Her Name: Resisting Police Brutality Against Black Women* (New York: African American Policy Forum and Center for Intersectionality and Social Policy Studies, 2015).

6. Ileana Jiménez, *Feminist Teacher: Educating for Equity and Justice* (blog), http://feministteacher.com/.

7. Freire, *Pedagogy of the Oppressed*, 17.

8. Nicholas C. Burbules and Rupert Berk, "Critical Thinking and Critical Pedagogy: Relations, Differences, and Limits," in *Critical Theories in Education: Changing Terrains of Knowledge and Politics*, ed. Thomas S. Popkewitz and Lynn Fendler (New York: Routledge, 1999), 62.

9. Chandra Talpade Mohanty, "On Race and Voice: Challenges for Liberal Education in the 1990s," in *Between Borders: Pedagogy and the Politics of Cultural Studies*, ed. Henry A. Giroux and Peter McLaren (New York: Routledge, 1994), 145–66.

10. Gloria Steinem, Presidential Medal of Freedom acceptance speech, November 22, 2013.

11. Burbules and Berk, "Critical Thinking and Critical Pedagogy," 62.

12. I have developed curricular materials for Hardy Girls and for SPARK that are useful in these moments. There are also other curricular materials and books with activities I use to facilitate the development of critical

consciousness with the girls I'm working with. These are listed in the resources section of this book.

13. Keertana Sastry, "Transcript of Jon Stewart's BS Speech from the Final 'Daily Show' Shows His Incredible Last Pieces of Advice," Bustle.com, August 7, 2015, http://www.bustle.com/articles/102772-transcript-of-jon-stewarts-bs-speech-from-the-final-daily-show-shows-his-incredible-last-pieces.

CHAPTER EIGHT: A WITNESS IN THEIR DEFENSE

1. An earlier analysis of this interaction can be found in Dana Edell, Lyn Mikel Brown, and Deborah Tolman, "Embodying Sexualization: When Theory Meets Practice in Intergenerational Feminist Activism," *Feminist Theory* 14, no. 3 (2013): 275–84.

2. Emma's interview and the analysis of this situation was first published in ibid.

3. Julio Cammarota and Michelle Fine, *Revolutionizing Education: Youth Participatory Action Research in Motion* (New York: Routledge, 2008).

4. Jeanette Winterson, *Oranges Are Not the Only Fruit* (London: Grove Press, 1997), 171.

5. Rich, "Vesuvius at Home," 157.

6. Kathrin Walker, "The Multiple Roles That Youth Development Program Leaders Adopt with Youth," *Youth & Society* 43, no. 2 (2010): 652.

7. Ibid., 651.

8. Gordon, "Gendered Paths to Teenage Political Participation," 33.

9. Ruth Nicole Brown and Chamara Jewel Kwakye, eds., *Wish to Live: The Hip-Hop Feminism Pedagogy Reader* (New York: Peter Lang, 2012).

10. Ruth Nicole Brown, "Mentoring on the Borderlands: Creating Empowering Connections Between Adolescent Girls and Young Women Volunteers," *Human Architecture: Journal of the Sociology of Self-Knowledge* 4, no. 3 (2006): 105–21.

11. Lev Vygotsky, "Interaction Between Learning and Development," in his *Mind and Society* (Cambridge, MA: Harvard University Press, 1978), 79–91.

12. Backbone Zone, poster collection, Maine Coalition Against Sexual Assault: http://www.mecasa.org/backbone/materials.html.

13. M. Howland and J. A. Simpson, "Getting in Under the Radar: A Dyadic View of Invisible Support," *Psychological Science* 21, no. 12 (2010): 1878–85; "Study Shows Social Support Most Effective When Provided 'Invisibly,'" video, http://www.youtube.com/watch?v=gp3j1vuOrEA.

14. Ivan Boszormenyi-Nagy and Geraldine Spark, *Invisible Loyalties: Reciprocity in Intergenerational Family Therapy* (New York: Brunner/Mazel, 1984). This notion comes from Nagy's contextual approach to family therapy,

in which patterns of invisible loyalties impact a relational context in ways that can enable or hamper aspirations and possibilities.

15. For a list of feminist organizations reaching out to youth activists, see the resources section.

CHAPTER NINE: "A POLITICS OF PARTICIPATION"

1. Celeste Montaño, "Google: Doodle Us!," SPARK Movement blog, February 27, 2014, http://www.sparksummit.com/2014/02/27/doodleus/.
2. The report, *#DoodleUs: Gender and Race in Google Doodles*, is available on the SPARK Movement website: http://www.sparksummit.com /wp-content/uploads/2014/02/doodle-research-summary-2.pdf.
3. You can watch the girls' "Doodle Us!" video here: https://www.youtube .com/watch?v=74UIdzTaWSk.
4. "This Could Be Google Doodles," Tumblr, http://googledoodleus .tumblr.com/.
5. Montaño, "Google: Doodle Us!"
6. Taft, *Rebel Girls*, 123.
7. Ibid.
8. Reagon, "Coalition Politics," 359.
9. Pat Macpherson and Michelle Fine, "Hungry for an Us: Adolescent Girls and Adult Women Negotiating Territories of Race, Gender, Class, and Difference," *Feminism & Psychology* 5, no. 2 (1995): 181.
10. Ibid., 183.
11. These workshop activities are available on the SPARK Movement website under SPARK Trainings.
12. Brown, "Mentoring on the Borderlands."

CHAPTER TEN: TRUST AND TRANSPARENCY

1. Maria Torre and Michelle Fine, "Researching and Resisting: Democratic Policy Research by and for Youth," in *Beyond Resistance! Youth Activism and Community Change*, ed. Shawn Ginwright, Pedro Noguera, and Julio Cammarota (New York: Routledge, 2006), 279.
2. Gordon, "Gendered Paths to Teenage Political Participation."
3. Taft, *Rebel Girls*.
4. Harris, "Jamming Girl Culture"; Taft, "Girl Power Politics"; Aapola, Gonick, and Harris, *Young Femininity*; Sharon Lamb and Lyn Mikel Brown, *Packaging Girlhood: Rescuing Our Daughters from Marketers' Schemes* (New York: St. Martin's, 2006); Roopali Mukherjee and Sarah Banet-Weiser, eds., *Commodity Activism: Cultural Resistance in Neoliberal Times* (New York: New York University Press, 2012).
5. Jessica Taft, "'Adults Talk Too Much': Intergenerational Dialogue and Power in the Peruvian Movement of Working Children," *Childhood* 22, no. 4 (2015): 465.

6. Natasha Blanchet-Cohen and Brian Rainbow, "Partnership Between Children and Adults? The Experience of the International Children's Conference on the Environment," *Childhood* 13, no. 1 (2002): 122.

7. Hava Rachel Gordon, "Allies Within and Without: How Adolescent Activists Conceptualize Ageism and Navigate Adult Power in Youth Social Movements," *Journal of Contemporary Ethnography* 36, no. 6 (2007): 631–68.

8. Ibid., 646.

9. This participatory action research is fully documented in Joanne Smith, Mandy Van Deven, and Meghan Huppuch's book, *Hey, Shorty! A Guide to Combating Sexual Violence in Schools and on the Streets* (New York: Feminist Press, 2011).

CHAPTER ELEVEN: SCAFFOLDING GIRLS' ACTIVISM

1. Maya and Treva's tip sheet can be found at Hardy Girls Healthy Women, "Tip Sheets," 2016, http://hghw.org/resources/tip-sheets.

2. Additional issues covered in GGE's curriculum, as supplied by Smith, are as follows: Building Community and Sisterhood; Identity, Oppression 101; Sisterhood Session: Voting and Civic Engagement; Identifying the Issue/Root Cause; Oppression and Power; Oppression and Privilege; Power Mapping and Analysis; Gender and Sexuality; Sexism and Patriarchy; Gender Based Violence; The Practice of Self-Care; Exploring Race and Racism; Movement Building; Women's History and Waves of Feminism; Introduction to Organizing; Consent and Healthy Relationships; IPV, Strategy and Approaches; PAR and Research; Exploring Class and Classism; and Visioning and Collective Power.

3. Women of Color, in Solidarity, http://wocinsolidarity.tumblr.com/post /10120129275o/mangoestho-so-ive-been-getting-messages-from.

4. Michael Resnick, "Thinking Like a Tree (and Other Forms of Ecological Thinking)," *International Journal of Computers for Mathematical Learning* 8, no. 1 (2003): 43.

5. Ibid., 44.

6. Kathrin Walker and Reed Larson, "Youth Worker Reasoning About Dilemmas Encountered in Practice: Expert-Novice Differences," *Journal of Youth Development* 7, no. 1 (2012): 18.

7. Resnick, "Thinking Like a Tree," 58.

CONCLUSION: WICKED PROBLEMS AND WILLFUL GIRLS

1. Horst W. J. Rittel and Melvin M. Webber, "Dilemmas in a General Theory of Planning," *Policy Sciences* 4 (1973): 155–69; Jon Kolko, *Wicked Problems Worth Solving: A Handbook and a Call to Action* (Austin, TX: Austin Center for Design, 2012).

2. Sadler, "TEDification Versus Edification," 27.

3. hooks, "Dig Deep: Beyond Lean In."

4. Maxine Greene, *Releasing the Imagination: Essays on Education, the Arts, and Social Change* (New York: Jossey-Bass, 1995), 5.

5. Sara Ahmed, *On Being Included: Racism and Diversity in Institutional Life* (Durham, NC: Duke University Press, 2012), 186–87.

6. Angela Duckworth describes grit in her 2013 TED talk, "The Key to Success? Grit," TED, http://www.ted.com/talks/angela_lee_duckworth _the_key_to_success_grit?language=en.

7. Ibid.

8. Paul Gorski, *Reaching and Teaching Students in Poverty: Strategies for Erasing the Opportunity Gap* (New York: Teachers College Press, 2013).

9. Bettie, "Women Without Class," 110.

10. Rebecca Solnit, *Hope in the Dark: Untold Stories, Wild Possibilities* (New York: Nation Books, 2005), 81.

11. Judith Butler, *Precarious Life: The Powers of Mourning and Violence* (London: Verso, 2006), 23.

12. Sara Ahmed, "Feminist Killjoys (and Other Willful Subjects)," *Scholar and Feminist Online* 8, no. 3 (Summer 2010), Barnard Center for Research on Women, http://sfonline.barnard.edu/polyphonic/print_ahmed.htm.

13. Taft, *Rebel Girls*, 261.

14. Giroux, "Protesting Youth in an Age of Neoliberal Savagery."

15. Noah De Lissovoy, "Epistemology of Emancipation: Contemporary Student Movements and the Politics of Knowledge," in *Critical Youth Studies Reader*, ed. Awad Ibrahim and Shirley Steinberg (New York: Peter Lang, 2014), 544.

16. Ahmed, "Feminist Killjoys."

17. Jeanette Winterson, *Why Be Happy When You Could Be Normal?* (New York: Grove Press, 2012), 117.

18. Solnit, *Hope in the Dark*, 23.